Read This First

Read This First

*The Executive's Guide to New Media—
from Blogs to Social Networks*

RON PLOOF

iUniverse, Inc.
New York   Bloomington

Read This First
The Executive's Guide to New Media—from Blogs to Social Networks

Copyright © 2009 Ron Ploof

iUniverse books may be ordered through booksellers or by contacting:

iUniverse
1663 Liberty Drive
Bloomington, IN 47403
www.iuniverse.com
1-800-Authors (1-800-288-4677)

Because of the dynamic nature of the Internet, any Web addresses or links contained in this book may have changed since publication and may no longer be valid.

ISBN: 978-1-4401-6685-3 (pbk)
ISBN: 978-1-4401-6687-7 (cloth)
ISBN: 978-1-4401-6686-0 (ebk)

Printed in the United States of America

iUniverse rev. date: 11/11/2009

To Tara,
who has always supported my crazy dreams.

Contents

Acknowledgments

The idea for *Read This First* emerged from three years of Saturday morning conversations with John Wall, the intrepid host of *The M Show* and *Marketing Over Coffee* podcasts. Since 2006, John and I have held a standing phone call that usually consists of me unleashing a torrent of hair-brained ideas and John breathing practicality into them. Thanks for keeping me grounded, John.

The first version of this book was completed in December 2008. That's when I performed a gut-wrenching act for any Type-A personality—handing my carefully worded prose to someone else. But my longtime friend and brilliant editor, Deb Bartle, treated my fragile ego with the appropriate level of respect and tough love to make the process as painless as possible. Without her help, this book would still be languishing on some distant sector of my laptop's hard drive.

Thanks to Karen Bartleson, my partner in crime at Synopsys. Although she is my star "New Media pupil," her knowledge and experience have far exceeded those of her teacher. She has become one of the most successful bloggers in the electronic design automation (EDA) industry.

One of the first goals I set for this book was to analyze real world situations—a feat that would have been impossible without data and the permission to use it. Karen was also the driving force behind acquiring Synopsys's permission for me to use the valuable data required to complete Chapter 10. A special thanks, too, to Rich Goldman, Karen Bartleson's boss, for granting that permission. Thanks to J.L. Gray of the Cool Verification blog for also sharing his personal Web analytics information. By combining J.L.'s data with Synopsys's, I was able to produce a cross-blog audience analysis that, to the best of my knowledge, has never been done before. Thanks also to Corey Scribner, who shared access to Google Analytics for his very popular Web site, *Bacon Today*.

In addition to providing deep insights into the public relations industry, Mike Kilroy, vice president of Maples Communications, was the first executive to read the manuscript and then commit totally to the concepts in it. Today, he is bringing the power of New Media to all of his clients. Thank you for having so much faith in me, Mike.

The book's title emerged from a monthly breakfast meeting with David Jacobs, podcaster, blogger, and social media consultant for Connected World Media, LLC. While discussing the trials and tribulations of helping clients understand New Media concepts, he pointed to my manuscript and blurted out, "Our customers need to *read this first*!"

I am indebted to Ann Handley for writing the book's foreword. Ann consistently tops the list of the fifty most influential women in social media, and the impact of her endorsement cannot be understated.

There are so many "Synopsoids" to thank. Thanks to Ken Nishida for convincing me to move from business development over to marketing where I could pursue my passion. Thanks to Guri Stark for believing in me enough to give me my first job in New Media. Thanks to Godwin Maben for being my first blogger and sharing his success stories with me. Thanks to my New Media posse: Mike Hessler, Tao Long, Mica Merce, JC Varela, Ken Wetherell, Mike Demler, Navraj Nandra, Eric Huang, Meghan Le, Kathy Schmidt, Jennifer Tanabe, Rick Jamison, Jo McRell, Beverly Henry, and David Stringfellow. I miss working closely with you folks.

Thanks to my early manuscript reviewers who took the time to give me encouragement and critical insights—specifically, John Wall, C.C. Chapman, Mike Kilroy, Jeremy Vaught, Chris Brogan, Scott Spiro, Harry Gries, Jeff Greenberg, David Jacobs, Steve Webb, Debbie Graney, Dan Sheppard, Karen Bartleson, Bob Wright, J.L.Gray, Corey Scribner, Terri Tucker, and Megan Enloe.

Thanks to my RonAmok! readers and my Twitter followers. Your comments, tweets, and e-mails helped form large portions of this book.

Lastly, I need to thank my family who have sacrificed the many hours I was perpetually illuminated by the bluish glow of my computer monitor.

Tara, Bryan, and Stephanie, I love you.

Foreword

One of my biggest beefs is that so many business books are inherently unreadable. It's not that the ideas are garbage. More often, it's that the ideas are sound, but the writing is dreary and boring, rendering the task of reading the text a little like wading through mud. With a little effort, it can be done. But the whole experience isn't very pleasant.

When Ron Ploof asked me to write the foreword to the book you are now reading, I said yes right away, before seeing what he'd written. I agreed immediately because the book was to be about our shared passion of social media. And in part, I agreed because I was honored: Ron and I go back a long way—we grew up in the same town, went to the same schools, and hung around the playground with the same kids.

But more than that, I said yes because I knew Ron's writing well enough to know that he wouldn't produce a boring business book. Ron wouldn't—couldn't, really—write a book that wasn't engaging to its readers. When he e-mailed me the final draft of the book, I wasn't surprised to see that he somehow manages to knit into a business book about social media stories about the Boston Massacre, Johannes Gutenberg, Bambi, AK-47s, the Boston Red Sox, and a bit about cesspools.

It occurs to me that my job here is probably to talk more about what the book contains (its essential message) and less about how it's delivered (the writing). And perhaps that's true: So let me say that the book is aptly titled *Read This First*.

As Ron promises, it's a great primer for executives looking to make sense of New Media tools such as blogging, Facebook, and Twitter in a world where a business is no longer in control of its brand and its message. The notion of marketing your products or your services to your customers by interrupting them repeatedly through advertising isn't enough anymore, Ron reminds us, and this book draws a blueprint for doing business in a climate where your customers increasingly have a voice (and aren't afraid to use it).

At the same time, I'm compelled to heap equal praise on the way Ron tells his story—on how he delivers his message. Because in my mind, that's a huge benefit to this book, and a reason to choose it over many others that might rest beside it on the bookshelf. Here, Ron will engage you fully: He'll make you laugh; he'll cause you to think; he'll inspire new understanding and insights. Above all, he'll help you see how the shift in the business climate can offer you and your business critical new insights into your customers—and how that can boost your own bottom line.

So yes, *Read This First*. Read it because you'll learn a thing or two (or forty…).

But *Read This First*, too, because you'll enjoy it. And truly, I can't heap higher praise than that.

Ann Handley
Chief Content Officer, MarketingProfs (www.marketeingprofs.com)
Author, Annarchy (www.annhandley.com)

Introduction

11:01 a.m. Wednesday, May 14, 2008

The nervous voice at the other end of the phone line got straight to the point. "And so we've decided that Synopsys doesn't need the full-time services of a New Media Evangelist."

The words hung in the air as I faced unemployment for the first time in my twenty-three-year career. I drove home in a daze, trying to make sense of it all. I thought about the success that Synopsys was enjoying with respect to its New Media efforts. I thought about the plans that we had for the next six-to-twelve months. For some strange reason, I didn't worry about family or financial security—instead, all I could think about was how we wouldn't be allowed to finish the work we had started.

I wondered aloud, *How did this happen?*

I quickly pinpointed the exact moment that I had sealed my fate. Back in November 2006, after months of discussions with Synopsys's vice president of marketing, I was offered a newly created marketing position to help him bring New Media technologies into the company. That was precisely when I made my critical error.

"I have too many direct reports," he said. "Does it matter who you report to?"

Excited about the possibilities of leading a Fortune 1000 company into New Media, I answered a bit too hastily. "No," I said—and my fate was sealed. From that moment on, I was Synopsys's New Media Evangelist, responsible for changing corporate marketing. However, instead of reporting to the cause's champion, I reported to the director of the "Web Team."

For the majority of 2007, I found myself in a constant state of battle with all sorts of people, including Marcomm, Public Relations, Web Development, Information Technology, Product Marketing, and the general managers of Business Units—who doubted the value of New Media compared with traditional marketing efforts. Luckily, the vice president of marketing supported my charter, so a quick call or e-mail frequently resolved any problems.

Our efforts were working fairly smoothly until the day our visionary vice president was wooed away by another company. The moment he walked out the door in January 2008, two things happened: I lost my air cover and the folks with whom I'd been battling for the past eighteen months lost any outward incentive to support Synopsys's New Media efforts.

The adoption and successful implementation of New Media technologies require an executive-level understanding of the differences between New and Traditional Media. Success depends upon a fundamental understanding of the types of content best suited to each medium. Success hinges not only on a sympathetic understanding of the perceived threats that New Media presents to traditional marketers, but also upon executive-level support.

I had failed to educate Synopsys's management about these issues. Without the words to explain New Media to my boss, how could I expect her to explain it to hers? When she was forced to make budget cuts within her "Web Team," what ammunition could I have given her to defend the company's need for someone dedicated to all things New Media? *This* is the book that I wish I could have handed to her. This is the book that I wished she could have handed to her boss, her boss's boss, and even the CEO. This book explains what New Media is, what it isn't, and how to make crucial business decisions with respect to it.

◆　　　◆　　　◆

I first thumbed through *The Cluetrain Manifesto* at a Barnes & Noble in early 2001, and the more I read, the more the book spoke to me. I'd spent my entire career in front of customers and, over the years, had developed a love-hate relationship with my various marketing departments. Their communications (presentations, brochures, white papers, etc.) lacked an essential ingredient—a reason for my customers to care. The language used in their canned presentations, McPressReleases, and tired old datasheets was, for all intents and purposes, empty and devoid of any human qualities.

That's when I read the first three *Cluetrain* theses:

1. Markets are conversations.
2. Markets consist of human beings, not demographic sectors.

3. Conversations among human beings *sound* human. They are conducted in a human voice.

I didn't have to read any further to make a purchasing decision. These three theses encapsulated everything that I had never been able to articulate to my marketing departments. I devoured *Cluetrain* in less than twenty-four hours. When asked to present my business development methods to an international audience of my peers, I leaned heavily on *Cluetrain* to create "Expanding the Conversation," a presentation about gaining customers' trust while remaining indispensable as a consultant. The presentation was so well received that it was requested and delivered many times over the next five years—all inspired by this insightful book that I accidentally stumbled upon while killing time in a bookstore.

Cluetrain was well ahead of its time even though it described how conversations were moving online, because the technologies of the day couldn't support them very well. Three years later, though, breakthroughs in Web-based technologies eliminated that bottleneck, and online conversations thrived. Some called it Social Media. Others called it Web 2.0 or New Media. The names are less important than what they represent—a collection of free Web-based tools that enable markets as online *conversations*. These tools, which carry odd names such as blogs, podcasts, online video, Facebook, Twitter, or del.icio.us, give ordinary people extraordinary power to create content, to network, and to share ideas with a worldwide audience—free of charge! Moreover, with few barriers to entry, these New Media technologies have radically changed the world of business communications.

Prior to 2004, the goal of a marketing organization was to deliver *the* corporate message to the marketplace. Post-2004, that message was being diced, sliced, and manipulated by online communities of passionate people who possessed the necessary tools to discuss the message's merits. Traditional marketers watched in horror as these online conversations proceeded with or without their participation or consent.

Today, companies fall into two categories: those embracing online conversations and those ignoring them. Those that choose the latter will continue to pump out controlled and obsequious content that will be ignored, eviscerated, or, occasionally, extolled online. On the other hand, companies that engage with these communities will gain skills and insights that not only increase their bottom line, but will also help them to create better products and boost profits.

The transition isn't easy. In order to adopt some of these methods, corporate executives must rethink traditional marketing and public relations roles. They'll be forced to look outside of these traditional content-creation departments to find new voices—ones that may emerge from unexpected places such as sales, customer support, engineering, or end-customers themselves. Such radical changes require tough executive decisions.

Read This First offers a game plan for decision makers; it outlines a top-down understanding of the online world. It is *the* book that executives should read *before* engaging with New Media. It is the *first* book that they should read *before* asking their public relations firms to explore this new realm. It is the *first* book that they should read *before* attending a marketing meeting—whether the presenter is extolling the virtues or downplaying the value of New Media. This book is designed to be a foundation on which to make executive decisions on how, why, and when to use New Media.

Choosing *any* New Media technologies will draw the praise of some and the scorn of others. But if I've done my job correctly, you'll have a roadmap that guides you around the landmines of New Media, while simultaneously helping your company's bottom line.

Ron Ploof
Aliso Viejo, California
ronploof@gmail.com

Chapter One

The Economics of Influence

o o o o o o o o o o o o o o o o o o o o o o o o o o o o o o o o o o o o o

Freedom of the press is limited to those who own one.

—*A.J. Liebling (1904–1963)*

I begin many of my speaking engagements by presenting the illustration in Figure 1-1 and asking if anyone recognizes it. Do you? More often than not, an American in the audience identifies it as "The Boston Massacre," correctly referring to an incident that occurred on March 5, 1770. But there is much more to the story than meets the eye.

The word "massacre" conjures images of defenseless citizens being cut down by ruthless aggressors and careful examination of the print reveals details consistent with that conclusion. Seven British soldiers are firing expertly leveled muskets toward a group of innocent colonists. Behind these soldiers stands their maniacal-looking commanding officer, sword raised as if giving them the order to fire. Faneuil Hall has been renamed "Butcher's Hall," and, to really pull at the heartstrings, a cute puppy looks on in disbelief.

The problem is that virtually none of it is true. A criminal trial of the soldiers determined that the incident was one of self-defense instead of a massacre.

Why would one of the most recognizable illustrations from the American War for Independence—one contained in the majority of American history books—be inaccurate? Why, 250 years later, would it still be recognized as a massacre instead of an act of self-defense? Simple. Because self-defense didn't serve the purposes of those, such as Samuel Adams, who sought independence from the Crown.

Figure 1-1: The Boston Massacre

Adams understood that those who controlled the flow of information to the masses could exert influence over them. With access to the city's largest printing presses, he exploited this power to successfully stoke the fires of a revolution. He, and others sympathetic to the cause, commissioned Paul Revere to create a poster to commemorate the event. Entitled "The Bloody Massacre," the illustration met the cause's requirements—its content can be more accurately described as inflammatory propaganda than historical fact. However, its influence didn't stop with eighteenth-century Americans. Two-hundred-fifty years later, an argument can be made that this print is the most effective public relations campaign in American history. And it all happened because of the printing press. It all happened because of the *Economics of Influence*.

The Economics of Influence

- When Johannes Gutenberg introduced the printing press to the West in the mid-1400s, he set into motion a means for future businesses to create and distribute ideas through the use of ink and paper.
- When Thomas Edison recorded sound onto a vinyl cylinder, he set into motion a means for businesses to create and distribute recorded sound.
- When Guglielmo Marconi transmitted his voice wirelessly through the use of electromagnetic waves, he set into motion a means for businesses to create and distribute radio and television signals.

These three innovations share a common feature: the costs associated with operation limit ownership to a handful of people with sufficient financial resources to do so. When it came to the creation and distribution of content, the world was separated into two publishing categories: the haves and the have-nots. This division transcended the monetary power of traditional socioeconomic classes—those with the capacity to create and distribute information also maintained a powerful influence over the hearts and minds of the vast majority that didn't. This power affected two groups, society and business, yet each reacted in opposite ways.

First, governments around the world were leery about the concentration of such influence into a minority of hands, and therefore passed laws restricting it. In Communist and dictatorial countries, governments often seized control of the media, using its influence to spoon-feed the populace with carefully crafted, state-sponsored messages. On the other hand, in countries supporting free speech, a more moderate approach prevailed as governments attempted to limit influence through licensing.

In the United States, Congress passed the Communications Act of 1934. The law has not only held up for seven decades—it's been updated numerous times, including 1996, 2005, and 2006. Rather than attempting to control the content, which would violate freedom-of-speech laws, the federal government licensed the electromagnetic spectrum, placing certain restrictions on media ownership. For example, by setting limits on the number of newspapers, radio stations, and television stations that any single publisher may own in any given market, the government could limit a publisher's influence within that given market.

Unlike the government, the business world didn't see this concentration of influence as a problem. Rather, businesses saw it as an opportunity to deliver their messages to large numbers of potential customers. Therefore, while governments sought to limit the influence of publishers, businesses sought to harness their influence.

By focusing on the markets that their messages could reach through the media, businesses created *marketing*, a corporate branch dedicated to delivering product and service messages to potential customers. Marketers approached publishers seeking to insert their messages into publications. Publishers countered the request with a proposition. If businesses were willing to pay for that access, publishers would be more than happy to sell column inches or broadcast minutes to do so. Subsequently, the *advertising industry* and Madison Avenue were born.

However, a critical element was missing from the relationship. Publishers needed more than advertisements to increase their audiences, which demanded compelling content and news. Simultaneously, businesses sought alternative ways to reduce the cost of delivering their messages. Publishing's need for content combined with business' need for cheaper access, culminated in the creation of another new profession called *public relations*. Businesses hired employees skilled in the art of influencing, and gave them the job of convincing publishers to talk about their companies for free. Over time, they perfected the press release—a document designed to assist journalists looking for "newsworthy" stories.

Thus began the love/hate relationship between publishers and businesses. On one hand, businesses preferred to have their stories covered by publishers for free. On the other hand, media companies needed newsworthy stories, but also needed to sell advertising space in order to defray costs. As a result, a game of cat and mouse ensued between journalists and PR professionals.

Publishers and Consumers Go Deaf

As the economy grew exponentially, so did the number of public relations professionals, and it didn't take long for their numbers to vastly outnumber those of the publishers. Press releases deluged fax machines and e-mail accounts, totally overwhelming publishers, who in a failed attempt to extract news-needles from press release-haystacks, found themselves overwhelmed by the sheer volume of information thrown at them.

What did marketers and PR people do to help their publishing brethren? Did they try to invent more efficient ways of getting the publishers' attention? Did they try to work with the publishers, helping them sift though the vast piles of self-described news? Nope. Faced with a deaf recipient, businesses did the only thing that they could conceive of doing—they grabbed their megaphones and cranked up the volume. The reaction was circular and comical. The more noise businesses made—the more deaf the publishers became. While marketing and PR people invested in louder megaphones, publishers simply got better at tuning them out.

Benjamin Franklin, ironically a very successful publisher himself, once said, "The definition of insanity is doing the same thing over and over and expecting different results." His two-century-old statement couldn't be truer today as corporate megaphones blare unceasingly.

While publishers were dealing with the constant bombardment of press releases, Joe Sixpack found himself of the target of marketing megaphones. Marketers used interruption techniques to distinguish their companies from the sea of sameness—their messages blared from radios while consumers brushed their teeth. They enticed consumer's eyes with newspaper ads while they drank their coffee. Drive times were filled with more jingles than Top 40 songs. Under the guise of "opting-in," marketers filled work and e-mail boxes with spam, hit them one more time on their drive home, and completed their messaging as consumers dozed off in front of their television sets. No place was safe from the assault. Over the years, marketers have placed their messages on bathroom stalls, movie theater screens, baseball hats, T-shirts, and Internet search results. Consumers have no safe place to cast their gaze or lend their ears without encountering advertising messages.

Economics of Advertising

Publishers and consumers weren't the only folks who were unhappy with the unintended consequences of communications. Business executives struggled with the effectiveness of their advertising investments. For years, marketers have convinced C-level management that a tiny percentage of a large number is a good thing. A 1 percent rate of return, something that would be laughed at in the financial industries, is applauded in marketing circles.

The reality is that advertising, by its very nature, is inefficient. Advertising is a probabilistic business solution, with no guarantee that anyone will ever read, hear, or watch the content that your company has produced. However, by combining the law of large numbers with delivering a corporate message and by placing that advertisement in front of a million people, the odds are that someone will actually read, look at, or listen to it.

The fundamental principles of the Economics of Influence state that the goal of any broadcast medium is to harness the power of large numbers and probability to make it worthwhile for a business to fund advertising budgets. The more attention that the medium delivers, the more likely it is that your company will reach a potential customer. In addition, the odds of reaching customers are getting smaller by the day. Marketing's relentless pursuit of potential customers has backfired with an unintended consequence. Consider the fact that customers are arming themselves with tools such as TiVo and digital video recorders (DVRs) (now leased or purchased from the very same cable companies that continue to sell advertising minutes based upon viewer demographics) to escape advertising and the situation starts to resemble a warped episode of *Spy vs. Spy.*

Access as a Scarce Resource

In a nutshell, the economics of influence has created a situation where:
- Media companies pay lots of money for their respective content and distribution methods. Print companies pay for paper, postage, and gasoline. Music publishers pay for manufacturing, packaging, and shelf space. Radio and television stations pay for licenses, transmitters, satellites, and broadcasting towers.
- Governments on the left *and* the right seek to restrict unapproved influence. Some regulate the broadcast frequencies. Others offer guidelines for what's acceptable to publish and what's not. Lastly, the more controlling governments allow only their own state-sponsored content.
- Advertising resembles a squirrel climbing a greased pole. With enough time and effort, he'll eventually get to where he wants to go, but it'll take more time and effort than he planned.
- Businesses want access to vast audiences for minimal cost. If only there was a way to be more efficient in targeting the messages as opposed to the traditional spray-and-pray methodology.
- Businesses bombard the press with often-worthless releases every day and the press can't keep up. As a result, companies are frustrated that

their "news" isn't getting covered and the press is frustrated that their e-mail inboxes are packed with volumes of drivel.

- Finally, businesses *and* content providers inundate customers with messages—from the minute they wake to the sound of the clock radio to the moment they fall asleep with the TV on. Weary consumers are embracing TiVo and DVRs, where they can use their opposable thumbs to fast-forward through Viagra commercials.

All of these behaviors were driven by the fact that the power of influence was held tightly within the hands of a select few. Access to vast audiences was considered a scarce resource to be divided among the few who could afford a seat at the table. However, a funny thing happened on the way to the office between 2000 and 2005. A new set of technologies began emerging that transformed a scarce resource into an abundant one. Armed with these new technologies, a new breed of content creators emerged to challenge those who controlled the influence.

The Perfect Storm

In 1995, the World Wide Web became a prevalent part of mainstream business. Web sites from every conceivable industry sprung up as businesses experimented with a new way to publish their marketing materials. Newspapers put their content online, and tech-savvy individuals began creating their own personal Web pages.

Between 1995 and 1999, this trend continued, as people got more and more familiar with HTML (Hypertext Markup Language), the language of the Web. Internet Service Providers (ISPs) reacted to growing demands from these new publishers by creating more robust services. Competition forced lower rates, further fueling the number of companies and individuals that published their content online. Although this love affair with online publishing grew, three bottlenecks remained to restrict the free flow of information between online publisher and online content consumer.

1. Hand-coding HTML pages was way too geeky for the average user.
2. There was no way to syndicate online content.
3. The more successful an online publisher became and the more hits the site received, the more it had to pay for bandwidth.

The first bottleneck was eliminated in October 1999 by a company called Pyra, which released a new "Web log" service. Through the company's innovation, anyone with access to a Web browser could publish their thoughts online for free. Better yet, publishing suddenly didn't require a degree in computer science. Pyra's publishing platform—"Blogger"— lowered the barrier-to-entry for online publishers who needed no money and a minimal amount of technical savvy to display their craft.[1] Anyone with the ability to type and press an upload button could become an online publisher. Blogger solved the first of the three bottlenecks, but these new publishers still didn't have a way to automatically distribute their content to their audience.

Newspapers are delivered to your door, magazines come in the mail, and radio programs come through the air. However, if I wanted to read my favorite blog, I had to manually point my browser to the Web site to check for new material. In the fall of 2002, a new technology arrived that allowed online publishers to syndicate their content to readers. Really Simple Syndication[2] (RSS is covered in more detail in Chapter 2) is a result of Web-syndication research that goes as far back as 1995 to Apple Computer's Advanced Technology Group. The technology didn't hit mainstream adoption until Dave Winer released a specification for RSS 2.0 in September 2002, which was subsequently used for the first time by the *New York Times* two months later. RSS provided publishers a way to deliver their content to online customers automatically. Although the technology required some geekiness on both ends of the channel—publishers needed to know how to create RSS feeds and consumers needed to know how to receive them—it was validated through the *New York Times'* adoption, which in turn fueled its popularity. Finally, with the ability to syndicate their content around the world, online publishers had almost achieved the Holy Grail of publishing—the ability to cost-effectively deliver their content to self-selecting audiences.

One last bottleneck remained. The cost of delivering online content, especially rich media (audio/video), was expensive. Unlike radio or television stations, where broadcast costs are fixed no matter how many people are tuned-in, bandwidth (delivery) costs for online publishers increase with audience size. As the demand for online content grew, popular online

---

[1]   Blogger was purchased by Google in 2003.

[2]   RSS stands for Really Simple Syndication that we'll describe in more detail in Chapter 2. For now, just consider RSS as a way that publishers can distribute content to their customers who specifically request it.

publishers found themselves victims of their own success—burdened with constantly crashing sites or paying significantly high bandwidth costs. In the early days of podcasting, 2004–2005, popular podcasters could easily exceed their Web host's monthly bandwidth allocation, thus forcing them to deal with one of two unpleasant situations: their hosting provider would either shut down their Web site or, even worse, they'd send the podcaster an invoice for the bandwidth that had exceeded their monthly allotment—a sum that could hit several thousand dollars![3]

The final innovation—fixed-cost distribution—ultimately opened up a new era in online publishing. In November 2004, Libsyn (which would eventually become Wizard Media) began offering unlimited amounts of bandwidth for a fixed monthly fee to rich media publishers. Libsyn's most economical option began at only five dollars ($5.00 U.S.) per month. By converting online delivery expenses from variable to fixed costs, Libsyn's innovative business model opened up a new era in publishing.

User-friendly publishing platforms + Web syndication + fixed bandwidth costs = New Media Revolution

---

The Economics of Influence Turned On Its Ear

In Paul Zane Pilzer's 1990 book *Unlimited Wealth*, he describes how traditional economics theory is based on a premise that wealth is created through the division of scarce natural resources. However, Pilzer reveals that the premise is bogus because it doesn't take into account the technology of the day, which defines what a resource is.

For example, according to traditional economic theory, a printing press is considered a scarce resource. It has a cost and must be housed somewhere. It needs ink, paper, and a team of people to run it. What happens when someone invents zero-cost printing that occupies no space, requires no ink or paper, and costs nothing?

That's exactly what happened in 2004 and, as a result, the communications game has changed forever. Perplexed traditional publishers watched online-only publishers chip away at their scarcity-based business models. Unencumbered by production and distribution costs, these New Media

---

[3] A podcast is an online audio program that listeners can subscribe to using the RSS technology that we'll discuss in Chapter 2.

publishers have turned the traditional publisher's scarcity-based advantage into an abundance-based liability. With this change, longstanding and seemingly untouchable publishing rules adhered to by journalists, PR professionals, and marketers are now being questioned, evaluated, stretched, and, in some cases, discarded.

Businesses, on the other hand, always need competitive advantages and shouldn't view a new communications model as a disaster the way that mainstream publishers have. No longer relegated to begging for a publisher's attention, companies now have the opportunity to communicate directly with their customers. Mike Kilroy, vice president of public relations for Maples Communications, says that online media has given businesses "everything that they've ever wanted"—the ability to communicate through their own, unfiltered, unedited, and straight-from-the-horse's-mouth platforms.

However, before businesses rush pell-mell into starting their own publications, they may want to remember the lesson of King Midas. Although he got his wish, he learned that too much of a good thing comes with a downside. Eliminating the publishing barrier-to-entry cuts both ways. If corporations can own a costless printing press, their competitors, customers, investors, and every angry citizen with an ax to grind can too. For the first time in history, both the press and businesses are finding themselves at the pointy-end of the quill, as those historically locked out of the influence game (readers, viewers, listeners, or customers) have joined the party.

New Media is changing the way content is created, distributed, interpreted, consumed, and paid for. Blogs, podcasts, and online video have made their way into our day-to-day language. Free tools such as Wordpress, Twitter, and YouTube are changing the rules of publishing forever. The communications rules that we learned in school and practiced successfully in business may now be liabilities within the democracy of the online marketplace.

This brings the conversation back to *you*.

As an executive, a business owner, a manager, an employee, or a customer, you must learn how to engage successfully with this new online marketplace. Your company has built its professional communications plans around skills developed to serve the *old* economics of influence. Those skills have served your company well, but due to the *new* economics of influence, they've become a liability that must be addressed.

The transition isn't easy. The proper adoption of New Media technologies requires one of the most difficult things for human beings—change. Many of the rules that govern corporate communications have become obsolete; others have skewed so much as to become unrecognizable. Fundamental assumptions about how to influence the marketplace must be challenged. As an executive, you need to ask yourself a very sobering question: does your company have the guts to honestly question *all* of its interactions? If so, this book is for you. If not, you might want to pass it along to the nice person who succeeds you.

Chapter Summary:

- New online technologies have initiated an inverse in the Economics of Influence—offering new ways for companies to deliver their messages to the marketplace.
- In addition to advertising and public relations, companies now have a third option by which to deliver their content—via New Media tools such as blogs, podcasts, and syndication of content via RSS.
- The marketing and PR techniques that worked so well in the old media channels don't necessarily work in New Media channels.
- Strong management is required to make a smooth transition to New Media channels.

Chapter Two

Listening Is Free

Anyone who doesn't spend at least an hour a day on search.twitter.com is making a huge mistake ... You can eavesdrop on every conversation in the world. And it's free.

—Gary Vaynerchuk

The largest New Media adoption hurdle that companies must overcome is inertia. It's easier for executives faced with new tools, new methods, and non-converging advice to choose inaction. The next two chapters will give you an overview of the basics—with just enough information to reach an executive-level understanding of the tools and how they can serve your business. If we're successful in that goal, you'll have a solid foundation with which to make good New Media management decisions.

Although there are thousands of New Media technologies—with new ones being added every day—each will likely fit into one of three categories:

1. Listening
2. Talking
3. Participating

These categories are listed in order of risk, from least to most. By learning about New Media in this specific order, your company will gain transferable skills, maximize the upside, and minimize the downside.

Listening Technologies

What are customers, journalists, investors, and competitors saying about your company's products, services, and attitude? To find out, most companies hire clipping services to gather marketplace intelligence. Specialists scour publications for keywords such as your company's name, industry, and competitors. Periodically, they summarize findings such as the number of company mentions and whether they were positive, negative, or neutral. Using this data, PR might prepare an executive report showing trends, measuring the success of past communications plans, or identifying future ones.

The whole notion of a clipping service was rooted in the old economics of influence and the printing press. After subscribing to an array of print-based publications, they combed through printed pages searching for keywords. If a match occurred, the article was clipped. When most information was distributed with ink on paper, clipping services were the most efficient way to learn what was being said about your company.

Times changed when the economics of influence forced publishers online—eliminating the number of physical publications that could be clipped. Human intervention was necessary for paper-based trade magazines, but it caused bottlenecks when searching through the thousands of new pages that are added to the Web every day. Computers could search, sort, and summarize online data much more efficiently.

As publishers shifted their content online, companies such as AltaVista® and Yahoo!® were formed to help people find information online. In less than fifteen years, search engine technology advanced enough for anyone with a Web browser to search for a keyword and be rewarded instantly with a list of relevant results. Online data increased, making it difficult for search companies to keep their databases current. Their most pressing problem was extreme diversity in content and composition. A new collaboration between search companies and publishers solved the problem by establishing guidelines to enable easy indexing of online content, which offered participating publishers better search results—from the minute the Web pages were uploaded! This collaboration proved successful for end-users such as your employees, who could find timely information when they wanted it. Put another way, because of this collaboration between online publishers and the search engines, your company gained access to up-to-the-minute reports of what the world is saying about your company, your CEO, your competitors, your products, and services—for free.

New Media Tip: Clip your clipping service

How much is your company paying per year for clipping services? Consider the pros and cons of saving that budget for something else and using *free* New Media listening tools that do the clipping for you.

One of the first New Media tools to emerge from this search engine/publisher collaboration is called Google Alerts™.[4] For the cost of the time it takes you to sign up for a Google® account (your company probably already has several), Google Alerts promises not only to track the same keywords that your clipping service does, but also to send an e-mail whenever those keywords are found.[5] Within five minutes of stuffing Google Alerts with a list of your favorite keywords, you'll have a customized stream of clippings delivered directly to your e-mail inbox.

Want to know the minute someone says something about your company online? Set the Google Alerts "How Often" switch to "as it happens." If that is too often for your needs, set the frequency to "once per day" or "once per week." As more and more publishers move online, your company will need automated listening tools to sift through the terabytes of fresh content uploaded daily.

Did I mention that Google Alerts are free?

I must warn you that a common theme runs throughout this book. The theme revolves around the fact that most New Media technologies require cashless investments—meaning that there's no reason to write a check for the technology. In fact, New Media technologies demand an investment dearer than cash. They require change and commitment—two things that most humans resist. Most people would rather throw money at a problem than actually roll up their sleeves and try something new.

Free online services only work when:

1. you support your employees' education on using the services; and
2. your company is willing to change its current method of doing things.

---

[4] http://google.com/alerts
[5] Go to https://www.google.com/accounts/ManageAccount; click on "Create an account now."

Without executive-level support, all corporate attempts to use New Media will be thwarted by those who refuse to change, and will ultimately fail. For example, if your PR director is enamored with her favorite clipping service, she's going to fight you tooth and nail about changing to a new service, regardless of savings.[6]

The new economics of influence require us to question fundamental business assumptions. When cell phones were prohibitively expensive, it didn't make sense for every employee to have one. The decision could be made with a quick glance at the bottom line. However, New Media technologies create an interesting dilemma for corporations. We don't trust innovations that increase productivity for nothing. With experience comes skepticism. Something-for-nothing always comes with small print.

The good news is that there's no reason to throw the old media baby out with the New Media bathwater. Want to hold onto your clipping service for a while? Great! Run a parallel test. Give one of your employees—preferably one who likes to try new things—the task of using Google Alerts to track the same keywords that your clipping service uses. At the end of the time period, compare the results—preferably right before you determine the following year's budget.

E-mail Inbox: The Cesspool of Personal Information

Google Alerts via e-mail is a smart way to gather competitive intelligence on the Web, yet it has an Achilles' heel—the fact that it sends results to your e-mail inbox. During the past fifteen years, e-mail, the killer app of the Internet, has become a productivity killer, as the average knowledge worker receives hundreds of new e-mail messages per day. As an information-gathering device, e-mail has a major flaw. It's packed with messages that share only one thing in common: the e-mail address of the intended recipient. Think about it. Where else can you find messages from such a diverse group of individuals—your boss, your co-workers, your spouse, your mom, and your kid's teachers? Where else can you find personal messages from friends mixed with business communications, frequent flyer programs, personal and professional newsletters, and meeting reminders? And if that weren't enough,

---

[6] Executive Heads-up. Your PR director may draw upon the "you only get what you pay for" argument. Beware. This is frequently a veiled attempt to protect next year's budget.

all of these messages are also smothered in a toxic dose of spam. Like it or not, your e-mail inbox is a cesspool of random content.

I call this phenomenon the "tyranny of the inbox." Each message competes for attention. And all messages aren't created equal; some hold unfair advantages over the rest. Take your company's newsletter, for example—the one that you just e-mailed to your customers, including Kevin. It arrives in his inbox with a dozen other messages, including the one from his wife. Which one do you think he's going to read first? That's the tyranny of the inbox—the fact that you as the sender cannot predict the context in which Kevin, the recipient, will read your message.

The e-mail-from-the-wife story is the nice example, because there's nothing keeping Kevin from reading your newsletter afterward. What if your message arrives simultaneously as his customer's? To make the situation more interesting, it's not just *any* customer; it's the one with whom he's been negotiating for three months. If he gets the deal, he'll be a hero. If he loses the deal, his company will be forced to lay people off. In this scenario, your perfectly written newsletter commands the importance of a hangnail.

If the other message contains good news, Kevin's day is made and a halo effect is cast upon all messages in his inbox. On the other hand, if it carries bad news, that halo effect transforms into a shroud, dimming everything else in his inbox, including your newsletter!

The tyranny of the inbox has nothing to do with the source of the content. When your company sent that newsletter, it did nothing wrong. However, if its arrival was tainted, your company will suffer repercussions—and you'll probably never know why.

As even more content moves online, we as consumers must deal with the deluge. You probably have three e-mail addresses: work, personal, and public. You have three voice-mail boxes: home, work, and cell phone. You read online newspapers and magazines. You watch videos and listen to your iPod®. You search eBay® for collectibles and check Monster.com® for jobs. Not only do all of these information channels compete for your attention, but they also require you to act to retrieve that information. You click on a URL or type it into a browser. And when you finally find what you are looking for, or worse, you don't, you must do it all over again, visiting another Web site, navigating through yet another page layout, trying to find the information that interests you. In the age of digital information, more time is spent finding and determining the relevancy of information than consuming it. With the prevalence of New Media, where anyone can be a publisher, the problem is only getting worse.

The good news is that help is just a mouse-click away. You just need to change the way you consume information online.

RSS: The Building Block of New Media

If your company is typical, your employees are drowning in a sea of information—with too much to read and too little time to sift out the crucial bits. They need help. You can provide them with a top-down solution.

A New Media technology exists that can automate much of the effort your employees spend wading through and consuming essential information. It doesn't require an advanced computer science degree, and it fits comfortably within anyone's budget. It's free. This wonder technology will:

- sift through tons of content on your behalf,
- extract only the information that you've requested,
- organize this content and deliver it to you automatically—totally eliminating your need to constantly check Web sites for fresh new content,
- sort this information into relevant buckets,
- and *won't* cost you a penny.

RSS—"Really Simple Syndication"—is the building block of New Media.[7] With it, your employees can construct a foundation upon which to build content consumption and creation strategies while you all benefit from increased productivity.

The best way to understand RSS is to find an area in your life that requires a persistent search, something that you are so interested in that you're always looking for data. Are you a sales professional with a constant need for information about your customers, prospects, and competitors? Perhaps you're a hobbyist searching services like eBay or Craigslist® to add stamps to your collection. While seeking information, look for an orange symbol like this:

---

[7] Unfortunately, the tools that will shape our lives are being developed and named by technologists. I have a theory that the adoption of new technologies would accelerate if a brilliant innovator paired up with a savvy marketer. Then, the technology could be described to normal people who wouldn't be intimidated by jargon.

It's called an RSS feed, and behind it is a powerful search capability that gathers the information that you want, the instant it appears, and presents it through a venue other than your e-mail inbox. Behind it lies a stream of information that you can subscribe to. Don't be thrown off by the word subscribe. RSS doesn't require payment for access; it simply means, "Send me *this*."

If you want to read the latest postings from your favorite columnists? Subscribe to their RSS feeds. Perhaps you find yourself searching Craigslist three times per day? The next time you perform such a search, look at the bottom of the page for the orange RSS symbol. A Feed Reader will notify you every time a new item that meets your search criteria is listed.[8]

Subscriptions to RSS feeds are the most important productivity tools that today's information workers can have.

Information Is Personal

In his book, *Being Digital*, Nicholas Negroponte notes that the value of information is in the eye of the beholder. For example, some information is very important to you, yet has no value to anyone else. Negroponte uses your refrigerator's contents as an example. What if your refrigerator could notify your car that you were out of milk? That piece of data has no value to anyone outside your household. Well, except for Sam Walton, who might envision what Wal-Mart® could do with the information. Rather than notifying your car, Walton could arrange for your refrigerator to notify the local Wal-Mart, which would automatically deliver a fresh carton directly to your door. The power of personalized search tools such as RSS is that the information it carries is highly relevant to you, the subscriber.

Now, I just need my refrigerator to read bar codes and create RSS feeds.

---

8   Feed Reader. This is an application that reads RSS feeds. Once a hard-to-find application, it is starting to become more prevalent. Both Firefox® and Internet Explorer® have the ability to read RSS feeds. MyYahoo® and iGoogle™ can also be used to subscribe to RSS feeds. My personal favorite is Google Reader™. All are good in their own ways, but most importantly, they get information *out* of your e-mail inbox, sifting out content to be acted upon.

A Business Example

What are your search requirements at work? Shouldn't you know if a customer announces a new product, promotes an employee, or goes bankrupt? What are others saying about your business?

The flexibility provided by New Media tools means that you don't have to bloat your e-mail inbox with results. Just as you can subscribe to an RSS feed of your favorite columnist or a persistent search on Craigslist, you can also subscribe to RSS feeds of search engine results.

Try Google News™ RSS feed: go to http://news.google.com. Type a keyword into the search box, something such as your company's name, a competitor's name, or an industry-specific term that you are tracking for a marketing survey. Press the "Search News" button, and Google will comb through more than 4,500 sources, listing all of the hits that it finds for your search. Are the results what you had hoped for? Too general? Tighten up the search terms. Too specific? Use more generic terms. Just right? Subscribe to the RSS feed for that search term and, every time that keyword or phrase occurs in one of those publications, your Feed Reader will be notified of the search results.

By subscribing to the RSS Feed, you'll be notified whenever your search criteria are met.

On the surface, subscribing to a Google News feed is no different from collecting reports from your clipping service. The information found is delivered to you. But scratching the surface reveals an opportunity that your clipping service cannot compete with—instantaneous, unfiltered access to live news and equally instantaneous ability to respond to it.

For example, at 11:06 a.m. on 9 November, 2007, I published a post to my blog *RonAmok!: The Adventures of a New Media Evangelist.*[9] The post described a company called dotSub and its tool that allows users to insert time-stamped subtitles in online video.[10] Only forty-four minutes after posting, I received an e-mail from Michael L. Smolens, founder and CEO of dotSub. Not only did he thank me for the post, but he also sent me his contact information and an offer to speak with me at any time. Obviously, Mark was subscribed to some sort of automated search technology.

Can your clipping service do that?

Okay. Can they do it for free?

---

[9]   http://ronamok.com
[10]   http://dotsub.com

RSS Meets the Account Manager

George Ortega is one of the best salesmen I've ever worked with. He has an incredible ability to assess a sales situation, understand the dynamics involved, and build a cohesive sales strategy. But computer technology has never been his strength. George used to sit in the office next to mine—where I was frequently needed to solve some Microsoft Word®, Excel®, or Outlook® disaster. So, I found it fascinating that the first salesman to walk into my office with a practical application for New Media was my friend, George.

George had attended an abridged version of my Social Media 101 class. Something that I said during that class made him ask, "I need to keep up with the latest news on all of my customers. Do you think that I can use Google Reader to do that?"

He needed to create reports about his sales territory. In order to pull those reports together, he had to visit many Web sites, gather the information, and then synthesize it into some mandatory PowerPoint® template. The synthesizing wasn't the problem—it was the time and effort spent searching for new content.

In ten minutes, George had signed up for a Google account and had begun building his personal RSS-based search tool. As he explored the results of one of his searches, a fresh news story popped up, describing how one of his customers was being sold to another company. Reaching for the phone, he thanked me for my time and said, "I'm sorry, Ron, but I gotta jump on this."

And that was it. Today, George has an elaborate RSS search system at his disposal. He knows exactly what is happening within his sales territory, and he loves to talk about it.

The Ultimate Eavesdropper: Twitter

In a speech before five hundred marketers, Gary Vaynerchuk, the social marketing genius from *winelibrary.tv* and garyvaynerchuk.com said, "Anyone who doesn't spend at least an hour a day on search.twitter.com is making a huge mistake. The free data that is on *search.twitter* is amazing. You can search anything and see what people are saying about it. You can eavesdrop on every conversation in the world. And it's free."

Twitter is an online service that at first seems frivolous.[11] Essentially, it is an online chat room that prompts its users to answer the following question:

---

[11] http://twitter.com

"What are you doing?" However, there's a catch. You are limited to 140 characters for your answer. Some people take this question literally, and you may find comments such as:

- *Just finished making hamburger stew and an apple pie. Ah, it feels like winter.*
- *Still stuffed from last nights donut incident. [sic] Think breakfast will be juice.*
- *Walking with my dog, Strongbad.*

But, frivolous is in the eye of the beholder. Every now and then you'll see an interaction such as the one that happened between a disgruntled customer and a vendor. On the evening of 22 May 2008 at exactly 7:15 p.m., New Media maven C. C. Chapman was watching the Boston Red Sox on his big-screen HDTV. However, there was a problem. The high-definition picture, which should have been flawless, wasn't. In his frustration, he sent the following message via Twitter:

> *@Comcast—Why is it that on any HD channel I get a line across the top of the picture? REALLY noticeable with sports.*

C. C. didn't expect anything from the message, he was just venting into the ether, no differently than he would if commenting to someone watching the game with him. That's when something interesting happened. At 7:16 p.m., exactly one minute after C. C.'s tweet,[12] Frank Eliason, who goes by the Twitter handle "comcastcares" responded with:

> *@cc_chapman If it is a line in one spot on multiple channels it is either the TV or the box*

Within a few minutes, a conversation ensued between a dissatisfied customer and a vendor. Had the conversation never happened, it likely would have festered, leaving C.C. with a bad impression of Comcast® and its services. Without Frank, if someone had later asked C.C. for his thoughts about Comcast, it's highly likely that he'd have negative things to say. But that's not what happened.

Their conversation resulted in a Comcast truck arriving at C.C.'s house the following morning to fix the problem. Today, instead of having bad

---

[12] A "tweet" is a message on Twitter

things to say about Comcast, C.C. has shared this great customer success story on his very popular *Managing the Gray* podcast.[13] By listening, Frank Eliason managed to accomplish what every company wants—to kill the customer support monster while it's little.

New Media Tip: Use active listening

Is your company listening to alternative channels for mentions of its name? Go to search.twitter.com and type in your company name. See what people are saying about you—instantaneously. Best of all, you'll never have to go searching for the information again. Twitter also provides a custom RSS feed for every Twitter search performed. Simply set up a search using the same keywords that your clipping service uses and then subscribe to the resulting RSS feeds. By doing so, your company will keep its finger on the pulse of instantaneous customer feedback. Free.

Chapter Summary:

- New Media technologies fall into three categories: Listening, Talking, and Participating.
- New Media technologies are frequently free of charge.
- Listening Technologies, such as an RSS Reader, can help keep your e-mail inbox clean of clutter.
- RSS (the ability to syndicate content) is the building block of your New Media listening strategy.

---

[13] http://www.managingthegray.com/2008/05/23/comcast-wins-with-twitter/

Chapter Three

Talking and Participating

○ ○

No matter what, the very first piece of social media real estate I'd start with is a blog.

—***Chris Brogan***[14]

The new economics of influence have opened the way for businesses to tell their own stories. In the past, corporate storytelling was constrained by budget and third-party interference. First, the amount of column inches or broadcast minutes that your company could purchase was limited by your advertising budget. Second, getting feature stories written about your company was subject to the preferences of journalists and editors. In the former case, although ads were expensive, you knew what you were getting. In the latter, although the outcome was free, getting your message out was a crapshoot, because at the end of the day, journalists always file *their* stories, not *yours*.

Today, businesses have exciting new ways to tell their stories in their own voices. Through the use of text (blogging), audio (podcasting), or moving pictures (online video), companies can use storytelling vehicles that were cost prohibitive only a few years ago. No longer dependent on others, companies can flex their creativity to tell the stories that they want, *when* they want, using the best medium for the job.

At this point, it's common for the journalism police to jump up and down claiming that companies will just say whatever they want, whether or not it's true—that they'll produce content so biased, nobody will read it. Let's

---

[14] http://chrisbrogan.com

be very clear here. Any company that tries to use New Media channels to spin the facts will end up hurting its online *and* offline reputation significantly. A checks-and-balances system exists, driven by the fact that your customers *and* competitors have access to the same New Media technologies as you. When companies use those technologies to lie, they get called out for it.

Talking Channels: The Blog

So far, we've identified two themes that run throughout this book: the economics of influence and free. There's a third. The largest problem that New Media technologies must overcome has nothing to do with their cost or functionality. By far, the largest inhibitor to the adoption of New Media technologies is the fact that they were named by technologists instead of communicators. The widespread adoption of these tools is inhibited by the unintended consequences resulting from the fact that propeller-heads named them.

Take the word blog for example. Derived by contracting the phrase Web log, the term doesn't necessarily roll off your tongue. A blog is like a journal, but instead of being written on paper, it's published on the Web. Posts are listed in reverse chronological order, with your most recent listed first. All posts are saved into a database—a fact which cannot be understated because *databases are searchable* and the more useful the posts, the richer the database that readers—both present and future—can consume. If readers of your systems-engineering blog are looking for a post on "how to model a rotary variable differential transformer," all they have to do is type those keywords into the blog's search field, hit search, and they'll be transported instantly to any posts that meet those criteria. However, that's not the most powerful aspect of having a database of indexed posts. If you write the best systems-engineering information on the Web, a user will likely find their way to your blog by typing the same question into Google.

Don't let the technology scare you. Although blogging tools are sophisticated content-management solutions, they require no more skill than a word processor.[15] If you can type and format things (bold, underline, or italicize), then you can blog.

---

[15] Wordpress is a popular blogging system that can be found at http://wordpress.org

Lastly, as explained earlier, blogs have a built-in capability to syndicate their content through RSS.

So What? Why Should I Add a Blog to My Web Site?

Most companies have Web sites consisting of a pretty homepage with four tabs on it: Company, Products, Services, and Contact. The content on these pages usually comes verbatim from a marketing handbook. Regardless of industry, process, or price—most company Web sites sound something like this:

> *We are a world leader in _____ ... we provide the best products and services ... blah, blah, blah ... we have the best customer support ... yada, yada, yada ... We are different because ... etc., ...*

Not only does the Web site say nothing, but also the ramifications are far worse, because even if visitors read the boilerplate, there's no reason for them to return. Since the content on the Web site never changes, why would anyone return to it? The obligatory company Web site is simply a repurposed print brochure dumped onto the Web; the only person who'll read a brochure more than once is your proofreader.

If your company has one of these static, five-page Web sites, the best thing that you can do is to add a blog to it and the reason is simple. Search engines are designed to find good content. The better the content, the higher the Web site is ranked in search results. Therefore, the best way to find your way to the top of search engine rankings is to add a good blog to it. We'll talk more about good content in Chapter 7, but all you need to know right now is that search engines such as Google, Yahoo, and Bing love blogs.

Talking Channel: The Podcast

Internet-delivered audio programming languished for many years until Apple® Computer released the iPod® in 2001. This portable media device changed fundamental assumptions about the portability of audio programming, offering users unprecedented freedom to take their entire music collections with them—whether they were in the car, at the gym, or climbing Mt. Kilimanjaro.

That's when a new breed of content creators began producing a new type of audio programming for portable media device owners who sought alternative listening experiences. Originally called "audio bloggers," these producers offered their shows via RSS subscriptions, giving listeners something that was impossible with earlier attempts to distribute audio via the Internet: an automated way to download new audio programming the moment it was published and the ability to listen to those programs at their leisure. Just as TiVo® had done with television, these audio blogs created a new genre of time-shifted audio content that, although playable on any portable media device, became known as podcasts, a term derived through combining iPod with broadcast. Today, companies can own their own audio channel by producing podcasts for their customers.

Talking Channel: Online Video

Once people started syndicating audio files, video creation and distribution was clearly the next step. But there's a big difference between distributing text—or even audio—and video: the file sizes that they generate.

Moving big files through the Internet requires bandwidth and bandwidth costs money. To illustrate the difference between the file size of text, audio, and video, this chapter fits into a file that is approximately 90 kilobytes. If I were to read this chapter aloud, it might take about thirty minutes, creating an audio file that would occupy about 30 megabytes—333 times larger than the text file! In other words, having 1,000 people download your thirty-minute audio podcast would require you to pay for the same amount of bandwidth as 333,000 blog readers. Online video files are even bigger—consuming about ten times more space than audio files. Therefore, 1,000 people downloading your thirty-minute *video* podcast would use the same amount of bandwidth as 3.33 million readers of your text-only blog! Libsyn had solved the bandwidth problem for audio, but another company focused its sights on video.

In February 2005, a startup by the name of YouTube® offered something previously unheard of: free video hosting. If that innovation sounds good, consider that the most important innovation wasn't reducing the cost of online video distribution. YouTube invented the delivery mechanism for the viral video, by allowing people to embed YouTube-hosted video into their own Web sites.

For example, if you were a blogger and wanted to post a video interview onto your own site without worrying about bandwidth costs, you'd simply upload the video to YouTube and then cut and paste a snippet of code into your blog. Instantly, your blog was transformed into a television station. Even though the video was stored on YouTube, visitors to your blog could play that video without ever leaving your site. In a YouTube-powered world, video-content creators could add customized videos to their own sites, while YouTube footed the distribution bill.

Have a video that is viewed one million times? No need to worry about the cost of distribution; YouTube has you covered. The simple fact that video producers can embed YouTube-hosted videos into their online properties is the reason why the company was sold for $1.65 billion to Google eighteen months after it was formed.

Talking Channel: Online Video on Steroids

So far, we've talked about the syndication of audio and video content to be enjoyed at the consumer's leisure. Time-shifted content puts the scheduling of media consumption into the hands of the consumer, who is no longer beholden to the publication or broadcast schedule of the content creators.

However, just as there's an advantage to time-shifted audio and video, a role still exists for the creation of "live" content. Free streaming services such as *TalkShoe*®[16] and *BlogTalkRadio*(SM)[17] help content producers around the world to broadcast their audio shows live. Want to take your programming to the next level and broadcast live video? Services such as *Ustream.tv* and *Stickam.com*™ allow anyone with a video camera, a Web browser, and Internet access to broadcast live video through the Web. Need to ensure that your entire sales team sees the live presentation, but only three people are available at that time? No problem. These services save your presentations to disk, so that those who missed the live presentation can watch the recording later.

How about getting even crazier? By combining a video-capable cell phone with a free online service such as Qik.com, companies can produce a live, remote, streaming video show. Is your CEO answering questions on a tradeshow floor? Grab your camera phone and broadcast it live. How about capturing a live interview with a Congressman from the steps of the Capitol?

---

[16] http://talkshoe.com
[17] http://blogtalkradio.com

Just do what U.S. Congressman John Culberson from Texas, does. Break out your Nokia® N95, fire up *Qik*[18], and start interviewing! The emergence of portable wireless devices with the ability to transmit audio and video is eliminating the need to park those CNN® trucks for the live satellite uplink. All your company needs is wireless access, a cell phone, and someone to press send!

Today, the process is still a bit clunky, but within the next few years, anyone with a cell phone will be able to live-stream video through the Web—and your company needs to prepare for it today. Is your customer support rep moody? Do you have rats in your kitchen? Is your supposed "green company" truck burning oil as it goes down the freeway? If so, it's only a matter of time before someone with a cell phone broadcasts it live where it will then be saved forever and discovered by thousands. In his book, *1984*, George Orwell had it all wrong about Big Brother. A few cameras won't be turned on the many. Many cameras will be turned on the few.

Participating Channels

So far, we've discussed New Media technologies that fall into two complementary categories: listening and talking. They're complementary because each technology sits at one end of a New Media channel. Talking technologies, such as blogs, sit at the head-end of the channel and send content to listening technologies such as RSS Readers, which sit on the tail end.

This section discusses a third option to the online mix—a multidimensional channel with multiple content creators and multiple content consumers collaborating with one another. This wide-open online cacophony is probably the most difficult thing for businesspeople to wrap their heads around—especially employees who are totally focused on controlling corporate messaging. This final New Media category is called *Participating Technologies*.

Participating Channel: Wikipedia®

A "wiki" is a piece of software that allows multiple people to collaborate on a new document. Named for the Hawaiian term *wikiwiki*, meaning fast, the

---

[18] http://qik.com/johnculberson

technology allows rapid collaboration across time and distance, as people from around the globe build an online repository of relevant information.

Many companies use wikis behind corporate firewalls to support large teams of people who need to share information. For example, let's say that your company has a multidisciplinary, international design team that is building the world's next best set-top box. Spread across geographies and time zones, they each need to contribute to the box's specifications, tradeoffs, functions, user manuals, etc. Rather than using e-mail and word processors to create the project documentation, the team shares all of its project-related information via a wiki. With a wiki, everyone is on the same page—literally!

The most famous wiki is Wikipedia, a highly controversial online encyclopedia that allows anyone to add articles to it.[19] At first glance, the idea seems preposterous. How in the world can people from all over the world with no real qualifications work together to build the world's largest online encyclopedia? For obvious reasons, the information can't be accurate, right?

Wrong. Although Wikipedia gets a bad rap from those who don't understand it, the truth is that it's an accurate source of information. The reason that it remains that way is through the passion of its users—who stand watch over their interests and monitor those entries to ensure accuracy.

Wikipedia isn't the Wild West that most people think it is. Rather, it's a community of content creators abiding by a strict set of rules. A Wikipedia article must be written according to three core principles:

1. Neutral Point of View
2. Verifiability
3. No Original Research

As long as you follow these rules, the content that you write is accepted by Wikipedia's fast-growing community. As of March 2009, S23 states that Wikipedia hosts 12.5 million articles in more than 250 languages that have been edited 661 million times by 16.4 million registered users.[20] Wikipedia is living proof that collaborative systems with passionate people working under simple rules work very well. All corporate executives need to understand its lesson.

Just like old media, New Media comes through different channels. Each channel has a different set of rules. Wikipedia offers a channel for consumers

---

[19] http://wikipedia.org
[20] http://s23.org/wikistats/wikipedias_html.php?sort=good_desc

to find information that is supposed to be neutral, verifiable, and doesn't have original research. If the content that your company produces contains any of those things, then it does not belong on Wikipedia. However, don't throw it away! It's just that your content will be better served through other New Media channels such as your corporate blog, podcast, or online video channel.

Lastly, your company must prepare for a unique phenomenon that occurs with regard to passionate people who modify Wikipedia pages. Even though nobody owns their Wikipedia pages and therefore nobody can control them, sometimes Wiki writers become emotionally attached to their edits, causing edit wars to erupt as the two parties swap edit-volleys faster than professional ping-pong players do.

Unless there are blatant factual inconsistencies, it's not advised to play the "last one with the pen" game. Instead, take a deep breath and choose your Wikipedia page battles. If your company becomes the victim of Wikipedia hanky-panky, there are appeals processes to follow. Just don't expect them to be resolved very quickly.

New Media Tip: Subscribe to your Wikipedia changes page

Want to monitor changes to your Wikipedia page automatically? Subscribe to the RSS Feed of all of its edits, which can be found through its "edit this page" tab.

Participation Channel: MySpace®

It takes less than thirty seconds for someone in one of my speaking engagements to hear the word MySpace and ask, "Isn't that the Web site where sexual predators lurk to gain access to my children?" I can't blame them. Open up today's newspaper or turn on the evening news and you're likely to hear about the evils of MySpace. That's when I usually deal with three issues immediately:

1. Yes, MySpace has sexual predators on it.
2. Children are smarter than you think.
3. People's compulsion to share information about themselves is something that your company needs to understand. If you don't, you'll be locked out of this very lucrative demographic forever.

MySpace is an online community built on participation technologies. For the cost of an e-mail address, MySpace users can create essentially their own place in cyberspace. Without any understanding of complex technologies, MySpace users can create highly engaging Web properties where they share information with their friends. Such information may include their hopes and dreams, the name of their latest crush, their favorite music, favorite things to do, favorite places to go, or their favorite products and services— quite possibly, your company's products and services.

It's the concept of friends that corporations must grasp. MySpace allows its members to control access to the content that they put on their pages. With a flip of a switch, MySpace users have a choice of opening themselves up to the entire world, or, as most savvy teenagers do, they set the switch to private, only allowing those people who they've *friended* (yes, friend is now a verb) access to their pages. So, if a MySpace user's profile is open to the world, everyone—from their grandmother to the sexual deviant down the street—can read and interact with the individual, yet if the switch is closed, only trusted friends have access to their MySpace pages.[21]

However, there is something hidden under this privacy switch, that frequently goes unnoticed. The MySpace-savvy individuals are using communications channels in a very different way than old media channels. Our kids are interacting, in private conversations, with only the people that they've invited into the room. Teenagers prefer communicating through services like MySpace instead of e-mail because if they've chosen their friends correctly, they can't be *spammed*. The next time someone says that the only way to get through to customers is through the house e-mail list, remind them of this fact.

Business executives should care about online communities such as MySpace because the most interesting conversations occur behind these closed walls. Since MySpace users have created safe discussion areas for themselves and their friends, they feel comfortable discussing things such as your products and services. They have no problem recommending that their friends buy this particular cell phone, that particular blouse, or avoid that particular energy drink because it has too much sugar. These conversations

---

[21] Instead of barring your teenager from using Social Media sites like MySpace, what if you make a two-part agreement with them. 1) They must lock-up their profile so that only friends can read and interact with them. 2) You get a MySpace account and they must add you as a friend.

are real and should mean a lot to companies who'd love to encourage their online communities to write about them.

Participating Channel: Facebook®

Facebook arrived on the scene in 2004 as a service limited to college students. In September 2006, it opened its membership to anyone thirteen and older, giving Facebook access to a wider user base. Rather than being a walled garden as MySpace is, Facebook offered its system as a platform to outside developers.

As a result, developers from around the world built applications that ran on the Facebook platform. They developed applications of every conceivable nature—from games to contact utilities to news generators, etc. Within a short amount of time, Facebook members could choose from a treasure trove of free applications that helped them customize their Facebook pages, find old friends, and connect with new ones.

The benefits that Facebook brings to individuals is apparent, but what about businesses? Why would corporations create applications for Facebook? What's in it for them? The distinction that executives must understand is that Facebook applications require users to accept licensing terms before installing them. By agreeing to these terms, they're likely giving your company permission to access their personal information, including demographics, their list of friends, and their Facebook-hosted conversations with those friends. If your company's Facebook application becomes popular, it'll have access to a valuable collection of Facebook-user data. Looking for males between the ages of nineteen and twenty-four who live in Montana, prefer R&B music, and read Tom Clancy? All you have to do is cull the database created through your popular Facebook application for the results to magically appear.

Facebook offers companies access to a rich collection of user-generated demographic information. Not only can Facebook users share their personal preferences, in addition they can, and do, create online communities for their favorite products and services—perhaps *your* products and services.

Do your customers share common interests? Facebook probably has a group where they gather. Does your company develop products for the iPhone-3G? A Facebook fan page exists that contains more than 500,000 members for your company to interact with. How about fans of your corporate brand? The Harley-Davidson® Motor Company has a Facebook fan page with more than 185,000 members. Do you have a favorite rock band from your childhood? The Tubes has a Facebook fan page with more than 1500 members. No fan page exists yet for your company? No problem. Create your own.[22]

The most important part of dealing with social communities is that your company must really understand how each one works. Just as Wikipedia has rules for content creation, online communities have their own unwritten rules for participation. If your company plans to participate in an online community such as a Facebook group, spend some time observing groups from afar. Be a wallflower. Look around. Listen to the conversations. Try to understand the overall language of the place. Learn their customs.

Then, *after* your company gets a feel for the rhythm of the conversations, ask yourself the following question: "How can we help make this community better?" Be useful. Seek first to help—even if (especially if!) it has nothing to do with your product or service. As members see that your company is willing to invest effort into the community, they'll likely reciprocate, in more powerful ways than you can imagine.

In his 2008 book, *Tribes*, Seth Godin describes tribes as people who gather together around a common identity. For example, individuals who buy big bikes, don leather apparel, and cover their heads with bandannas have self-identified themselves as members of the "Harley-Davidson" tribe. The first thing that companies must do before joining or creating an online place for their tribes is to do some research. The great thing about online information is that it is easy to monitor. Seek to answer fundamental questions such as:

- Which Social Media sites do your tribes prefer?
- What memes—highly charged tribal conversations—are prevalent within them?
- What are their tribal customs?
- How can your company become a member of these tribes?
- What are they saying about your company?

---

[22] It's also important for companies to do some research before creating a Facebook fan page. If your brand is popular, there's a good chance that not only does a Facebook place exist, but that many of them exist. Before jumping and creating a Facebook page that competes with existing ones, perhaps your company can join with one of the more popular ones.

- What are they saying about your competitors?

Once you have identified, studied, and understood the customs of your potential tribes, your company will be ready to engage with them. If you've done your homework, those who interact with the community on your company's behalf will clearly understand how traditional marketing messages won't work within the community.

Merrimack College Alumni Facebook Group

Merrimack College alumni relations officer Christina Doherty's job is "to engage with the young alumni ... those who've graduated in the past 10–15 years." The term made me wince, because I graduated from Merrimack more than twenty-three years ago and therefore by definition I must be part of the "old alumni." But I digress. As a tribal leader, she sought to find a place online for her tribe to gather. A Facebook group seemed like a natural fit.

When creating the group, Christina noticed that other Merrimack-related Facebook groups also existed, evidently created by former Merrimackans seeking to connect with past classmates, yet they had nowhere else to go. That's when Christina did something extraordinary—something that all organizations can learn from.

Instead of putting the Merrimack College Alumni Facebook group out there to compete with these other groups, she reached out to them, suggesting that they pool their resources and unify into one. She explained her role at the college and offered to take over the work necessary for maintaining the groups. Because of her offer, Merrimack alumni now have a much more robust online community. Christina duplicated the process when creating a LinkedIn® group—essentially unifying disparate profiles into a single Merrimack LinkedIn group.

Is your company trying to build online tribes that support your organization? Are these corporate-sponsored online communities competing with or supporting existing ones? Does it make sense to share resources for the greater good of the tribe? What if you find a very large and thriving group? Would your company be willing to take a support role instead of a lead role for the betterment of the group?

Companies looking to form online spaces for their tribes need to take a lesson from Christina Doherty. Find your online tribes. Then, reach out and take care of them.

In order to be successful within any online social community, companies must follow a simple rule: *Your company must add more value to a community than it takes from it.*

If someone asks a question about your company, answer it. If someone shares a customer-support nightmare about your company, reach out and offer to help. Seth Godin has a stark description of old versus New Media: pointing out that traditional marketers do things *to* people, while New Media marketers do things *for* them. Two tiny prepositions, yet one massive difference.

Lastly, after becoming a valuable member of an online community, your company will learn that not all tribal members are created equal. Some are more vocal. Others, perhaps even some of the less vocal ones, will actually be more influential. Companies must identify these tribal leaders and engage with them. Tribal leaders may take the form of bloggers, podcasters, or online video producers. They are content creators who use text, pictures, sounds, and video to connect with their own tribes. Reach out and offer to help them create their content, allowing them to describe *your* products and services in *their* words.

New Media Tip: Listen to what others say

What can your company learn from its tribal leaders as they describe *your* products and services in *their* words?

Do these passionate content creators need photographs or high-resolution logos? Provide them. Do they need front-row access at your latest user group meeting? Give it to them. By taking care of your tribal leaders, they'll take care of you and your brand.

The largest resistance to allowing external voices to talk about your products and services will come from those employees who are wedded to controlling corporate messaging. Consider this your warning. Their hysteria can trigger false alarms, and it's your job as an executive to keep them from derailing corporate New Media efforts.

We'll talk more about these *Traditionals* in later chapters, but it is your job to carefully consider the appropriate interaction with social media communities. Traditional marketers may prefer to use their war analogies to:

- *target* customers,
- *launch* initiatives at them,

- *orchestrate campaigns* against them,
- or *blast* messages at them.

But they need to remember that rushing pell-mell into social networks with traditional marketing guns a-blazin' will result with their companies at the wrong end of a firing squad.

Putting It All Together: Listening, Talking, and Participating

New Media listening, talking, and participating technologies offer a triple-threat for your business. By gathering up-to-date information about your business, telling your stories in an authentic voice, and tapping into online groups that are passionate about your products and services, your business has the ability to communicate the way that it's always wanted to, but never could before.

Chapter Summary:

- Companies need to adopt New Media technologies to publish their own content.
- Blogs offer a way for companies to create their own text-based publications.
- Podcasts and online video offer a way for companies to add audio and video to their message-delivering capabilities.
- Using participation channels such as Facebook and Twitter, companies have new ways to interact with their customers.

Chapter Four

Bambi's Got an AK-47

o o o o o o o o o o o o o o o o o o o o o o o o o o o o o o o o o o o o o

David put his hand into the bag and took out a stone, hurled it with the sling, and struck the Philistine on the forehead. The stone embedded itself in his brow, and he fell prostrate on the ground.

—*1 Samuel* 17: 49

Times have changed. Under the old economics of influence, those with the largest marketing budgets could cast their messages the farthest. Today, the proverbial New Media playing field is leveled, as anyone with a Web browser can talk, listen, and participate globally for little or no cost. The democratization of New Media communications channels lends voice to anyone with a message, whether that message is a glowing recommendation or a scathing rebuke, giving your PR team yet another reason to lose sleep at night. The question remains: *Is your company listening?*

What is the first brand impression that someone gets while doing a simple online search for your company? Give it a whirl. Perform a Google search for your company's name. Note that the results on your computer screen are identical to those found on your prospect's, customer's, and competitor's screens also. What does it say? All positive things? Congratulations, your company is either good or lucky. But dig a slightly deeper and see how else Google is representing your company to the world.

You'll likely find opinions about your brand. Some will love you. Others won't. You may find some news or someone's commentary on that news. You may find blog posts from people who've had direct contact with your company's staff. No matter what these results say, no matter whether they are true or not, there is only one thing that your company can do about it: determine how to react to the results.

Let's take Google for a spin to illustrate the power of search-based corporate reputation. On September 29, 2008, a Google search on the term "Walmart" revealed 39,500,000 "hits." And of those thirty-nine million, here were the top ten:

1. Walmart.com: Save money. Live better.
Shop Low Prices Online for Electronics, Toys, Home, Garden, Baby, Sports Products & More.
www.walmart.com/

2. Wal-Mart Stores, Inc.
Corporate information, jobs, stock information, and company history.
walmartstores.com/

3. Wal-Mart Watch
Wal-Mart Watch is a nationwide campaign to reveal the harmful impact of walmart on american families and demand reform of their business practices.
walmartwatch.com/

4. Wal-Mart - Wikipedia, the free encyclopedia
Wal-Mart Stores, Inc. is an American public corporation that runs a chain of large, discount department stores. It is the world's largest public corporation …
en.wikipedia.org/wiki/Wal-Mart

5. Thank you for visiting Wal-Mart
Thank you for visiting Wal-Mart Music Downloads. We are currently in the process of working on making this section of our site better than ever, …
musicdownloads.walmart.com/

6. WakeUpWalMart.com - Join the fight to change Wal-Mart and change …
US-based group provides research, action steps, and resources for community-based efforts around worker rights, local development, and foreign trade policy.
wakeupwalmart.com/

7. Walmart.com - Music Downloads
Walmart.com - Music Downloads. … edc-swap8.walmart.com /swap/index.jsp, /swap/ loadMain2.do, /swap/loadMain3.do, / swap/LoadThreeColumn.do …
downloads.walmart.com/swap/

8. Walmart.com - Free Samples & Trials
Create a new Walmart.com account. Enter your 13-digit order number: … The Walmart.com site includes Flash technology. To avoid interruption of software …
instoresnow.walmart.com/In-Stores-Now-Free-Samples-And-Trials.aspx

9. WAL-MART: The High Cost of Low Price
Official web site for the new film WAL-MART: The High Cost of Low Price. Features trailer, latest news and allows YOU to sign up and become directly …
www.walmartmovie.com/

10. News results for walmart
Walmart to pull plug on DRM servers - Sep 28, 2008
So, Walmart is to pull the plug on its DRM servers and leave all the suckers customers who bought DRM-encumbered music up a creek without a paddle. …
ZDNet - 24 related articles »

Although these results look like the simple compilation of a search engine, John Battelle, the author of *The Search: How Google and Its Rivals Rewrote the Rules of Business and Transformed Our Culture*, has another description. He calls Google a "database of intentions," because people using the search engine are intent on finding something. It may be a temporary or a persistent need, but nonetheless, they're looking for something specific. In Wal-Mart's case, if the searcher is intent on finding the nearest Wal-Mart store, a particular product, investment information, or believes that Wal-Mart pushed the local mom-and-pop shop off of Main Street, Google's top ten results have something for everyone.

Take a look at the top ten results. Of the top ten findings, exactly half are directly controlled by Wal-Mart. Congrats to the marketing department; they've done a great job. Wal-Mart's PR department, though, is probably looking closely at the other half. For example, the fourth item listed is Wal-Mart's Wikipedia page—a document that contains 8,198 words that were not authorized by Wal-Mart's PR department. Instead, people with a keen interest in Wal-Mart participated to create the fourth-most relevant online document about the company. The bottom of this Wikipedia page lists 110 references to other sources of information, including a hyperlink to the "Criticism of Wal-Mart" Wikipedia page. Ironically the criticism page contains 9,225 words—12.6 percent more than Wal-Mart's main Wikipedia page!

Let's dig even deeper. Returning to the Google search results, we can see that items three, six, and nine identify Web sites dedicated to grinding Wal-Mart axes. Item nine—"Wal-Mart: The High Cost of Low Price"—links directly to a bright blue squeeze page with the following messages in large white letters.[23]

"Breathtaking"—*New York Times*

"Mesmerizing!" —*Salon.Com*

"Two Thumbs Up!" —Ebert & Roeper

With a simple mouse click, a visitor can watch a movie trailer, complete with dark music underscoring helpless-sounding people who are blaming their economic predicaments on the all-powerful Wal-Mart. The two-minute-forty-eight-second video, hosted for free on YouTube, had been viewed 821,581 times over its first twenty-nine months.

As an executive, it's important for you to pause and think about this for a moment. How much money would your marketing department require to broadcast a three-minute video to eight hundred thousand people? But that's exactly what this organization did—for free.

If visitors want to purchase DVDs of "Wal-Mart: The High Cost of Low Price," they simply need to click on the Amazon.com affiliate link

---

[23] http://www.walmartmovie.com/

and purchase it for $9.99. (Yes, the producers are even getting a cut of their own Amazon sale!) If, on the other hand, they'd prefer to pass on the opportunity, but still want to "Join the Revolution," visitors may sign up for the organization's e-mail newsletter. And finally, in a bizarre twist on how much the new economics of influence have totally turned the world upside down, not only is the DVD being sold at the usual places such as Amazon. com® and Barnes and Noble, not only can it can be rented through services such as Netflix, but a visitor may also purchase this anti-Wal-Mart DVD directly from Kmart®—a direct Wal-Mart Competitor!

The point is that people have always been talking about your company's brand; they've just never had the opportunity to tell a lot of people about it. In the past, if I had a bad customer experience, I would tell a few sympathetic friends who'd listen politely and perhaps offer some emotional support. Maybe they'd tell a friend, who might tell another friend, and so on. But eventually the story would die, because word-of-mouth message propagation has a major flaw in it. Each time the story is passed from person to person, it loses steam until it no longer has the energy required to continue.

But along came New Media allowing people to tell *their* stories, in *their* own voices. Instead of the traditional word-of-mouth scenario, today's stories are being published to the Web, where search engines index them forever. Once a story is online, all viewers will see an exact copy of the original story, delivered with the same passion as the first time it was recorded. If they are moved to pass that story onto others, they can do so by simply cutting and pasting a URL into an e-mail—thus keeping the story alive.

Gary Vaynerchuk discusses the differences between the old and new word-of-mouth.[24] "The Internet is so different today than it was five years ago, it is scary. Word-of-mouth is on steroids ..." he says. "Here's why. Because now we have tools that let us keep pushing the conversation forward. The word is traveling."

For the first time in history, the consumer has a voice in the global economy. It isn't the first time that the consumer had such a voice. When all business was local, word-of-mouth worked extremely well. If a vendor at the local farmer's market had a bad reputation, everyone in the neighborhood knew it. If a business deal went bad, the news would spread throughout the community, fueling street corner conversations and Sunday homilies. But when the economy outgrew the confines of the neighborhood, the power of

---

[24] http://garyvaynerchuk.com/

word-of-mouth diminished, leaving only those with the financial resources with the ability to spread their messages to geographically diverse audiences. Before the advent of New Media technologies, bad businesses could hide in the global economy. But not anymore. Bad reputations now travel at the speed of light.

Bambi's Got an AK-47

The fact that others can tell *their* stories about *your* brand is a new reality for modern business, and most companies don't have the necessary skills to deal with it. Their traditional PR and marketing staff have skills developed under the old economics of influence, and therefore, they only know one way to play the game.

Control the message. Control the brand.

Control worked well when the marketplace consisted of a finite number of publications and journalists. If a newspaper published a bad review of your product or service, your company's PR folks rushed to the phones to contain the story, much like firefighters containing a brush fire. With the appropriate amount of spin and a bit of luck, PR might slow the story, just long enough to keep word-of-mouth from sustaining itself.

Yet, such a feat is almost impossible today as the concept of message control is an oxymoron. With cost-effective publishing platforms in the hands of everyday people, anyone with a video camera and a YouTube account can record "A Comcast Technician Sleeping on my Couch" where it has been seen more than 1.2 million times.[25] The same customers that businesses once targeted with their marketing campaigns; the same ones that companies blasted e-mails to; or launched initiatives at; are now armed with their own battlefield weapons. The hunted have become the hunters and Bambi's got an AK-47.

In the mid-1990s, as the World Wide Web was gaining in popularity, Owen Davis wanted to share his frustration with the local Regional Bell Operating Company (RBOC), NYNEX®. Finding a new way to amplify his voice, he created a Web site called NYNEXSucks.com. In it, he described the trials and tribulations of getting an ISDN line installed at his company.

---

[25] A Comcast Technician Sleeping on my Couch http://www.youtube.com/watch?v=CvVp7b5gzqU (Note: While editing the book, this video was taken down from YouTube according to the following message: "This video is no longer available due to a copyright claim by a third party.")

Had that been the extent of the online discussion, the story might have died right there. But it didn't. Others came to his site and shared their own NYNEX horror stories. Mr. Davis' Web site struck fear into the hearts of public relations professionals around the world as they were faced with a story that they just couldn't control.

So, how did NYNEX respond? Did it see Mr. Davis' Web site as an opportunity to engage in a conversation with disgruntled customers? Did it see an opportunity to learn from them—possibly to increase the quality of their telecommunications services? No. Instead, NYNEX saw his Web site as an attack on its brand and did the only thing that it could conceive of to rectify the situation by gobbling up all the domain names that ended in "sucks." A quick look at Whois.net today shows that NYNEXSucks. com, BellAtlanticSucks.com, and VerizonSucks.com are all owned by the RBOC's surviving entity, Verizon. The RBOCs executed an old economics of influence-based plan predicated on the belief that if one controls the distribution channels, one controls the message. By purchasing all of the domain names ending in "sucks," these companies bet that they could make the problem go away.

The plan might have worked had search engine technology not advanced to the point where it devalued the importance of the domain name. While Verizon spent all sorts of time and money collecting every combination and permutation of its name and "sucks," a stay-at-home mom using free blog-hosting thwarted their efforts.

On August 7, 2008, a Google search for "Verizon Sucks" yielded 18,800 hits, of which the top one, is a February 4, 2008, blog post entitled: "Very Unhappy with V3rizon!!"[26]

Does the hyperlink bring a visitor to a Web site dedicated to the destruction of Verizon? Nope. Instead, it leads to a personal blog called *Mama(e) in Translation*, written by a stay-at-home mom with a PhD. This single post is intermixed with her postings about everyday life, she just happened to release her frustrations upon Verizon. At the end of the post, the author offers a challenge to her readers: "Any horror stories to share? Bring them on because they're surely going to make me feel better right now!"

Twenty-seven people took "Mama(e)" up on her challenge, expressing their frustrations through their own Verizon horror stories. This single post—the one that's listed as the first among 18,799 others—demonstrates

---

[26] http://mamaintranslation.blogspot.com/2008/02/verizon-sucks.html

a clear example of the forces behind the new economics of influence. Did this blogger spend lots of money developing and maintaining her Web site? Did she need to register a domain name with the word "sucks" in it so that people could find her Verizon story easily? No and no. *Mama(e)in Translation* is hosted on blogspot.com, a free blogging service owned and operated by Google—the same search engine that indexed and ranked her post in the first place.

As an executive, you must come to grips with the fact that your company has lost control of its brand. It's gone. *Sayonara. Arrivederci.* The longer that your company denies it, the longer your PR and marketing folks resist this truth, the sillier your company will look. It's time for businesses to stop delivering spin-based messages to a group of online customers who are just snickering behind their backs. If Goliath doesn't acknowledge this simple fact, then consumers will use their new economics-of-influence slingshots and give him a massive headache.

New Media Tip: Enter online conversations

As an executive, it's your responsibility to lead your company to make good decisions. Instead of pretending that your company can control online conversations, it's time to find ways of entering into them.

Losing Control May Not Be Such a Bad Thing

So far we've talked about the negative effects of losing brand control. However, to be fair, there are positive aspects of losing control of your brand too. One such example began on Saturday, June 3rd, 2006, when Fritz Grobe and Stephen Voltz of Buckfield, Maine, released a clever video demonstrating the spectacular results of dropping 500 Mentos® mints into 101 two-liter bottles of Diet Coke®. [27] The video reveals two white-lab-coat clad gentlemen standing in an open field. They're surrounded by two-liter bottles of Diet Coke attached to all sorts of gizmos and gadgets. Entertaining music plays in the background as they pull cord after cord, setting off a delightful series of Diet Coke geysers that reach well over their heads.

The propulsive force behind this bubbly reaction is a peculiar process called nucleation, a rapid release of the bubbles from carbonated liquid that occurs after immersing an object containing a high surface area into it.

---

[27] http://eepybird.com/dcm1.html

The nucleation caused by dropping Mentos candies into Diet Coke results in delightful soda plumes that can shoot more than ten feet into the air. Online videos of this dazzling reaction weren't uncommon before Grobe and Voltz produced theirs, but the pair added a twist. The two, under the name Eepybird.com, orchestrated a complex fountain effect created by dozens of soda bottles that rivaled the waterworks displays at the Bellagio® Hotel in Las Vegas, Nevada.

The online video propelled these soda pop pyro-technicians into stardom as they performed their magic for the likes of David Letterman and Ellen DeGeneres. Their bubbly antics were mentioned in the *Wall Street Journal*®, *Rolling Stone Magazine*®, and the *New York Times*. And more importantly, these two men from Maine had become unlikely evangelists for two worldwide brands even though none of the parties, Coca-Cola®, Perfetti Van Melle®, or Eepybird had any official affiliation—yet.

Overnight, corporate giants Coca-Cola and Perfetti Van Melle lost control of their brands. On Friday, June 2, 2006, brand managers at Coca-Cola went to bed under the assumption that they were in the soft drink business. Their counterparts at Perfetti Van Melle woke up on Saturday morning believing that they were in the candy business. Literally overnight, each company found itself thrust unwillingly into the entertainment business. It's a lesson that every marketer must learn in the new economics of influence:

New Media Tip: Admit that you've lost control

The only remaining control you have over your brand is how you ***react*** to what others are saying about it.

Perfetti Van Melle embraced the entertainment concept almost immediately, promising Grobe and Voltz as much Mentos as they could consume, or nucleate, or do whatever they wanted to do with it. Coca-Cola, on the other hand, didn't warm up as quickly, taking several months to ink a deal. To be fair, who could blame them? One can only imagine the fits that Coca-Cola's legal counsel went through as they wrestled with the fact that when their universally loved soft drink is combined with a mint candy, that someone could end up losing an eye. In a litigious world, does it really make sense to encourage the conversion of your carbonated soft drink into a weapon of mass entertainment? The answer may not be as simple as it seems.

Floral Quarrel—A Case Study

Two days make or break a florist's fiscal year: Valentine's Day and Mother's Day. If that isn't enough to scare you away from entering the flower business, the following fact should—the majority of those orders come within twenty-four hours of the dates. Look up "logistical nightmare" in the dictionary, and you are likely to find a picture of a florist's calendar with these two dates circled in red.

And so on February 13, 2008, I—along with half of America—tried to place an order for flowers to be delivered the following day. What I didn't expect to find was a New Media story. It's a story of a $19 billion industry that's wrestling with the realities of an online world. It's a story about one disgruntled customer and four flower vendors. Two of these vendors are large international companies, and the remaining two are mom-and-pop shops. Two of the vendors are using New Media for competitive advantage, while the other two are grappling with the fact that they've lost control of their brands.

Our story begins with the roses that I had ordered never arriving, even though a "confirmation-of-delivery" e-mail from 1-800-Flowers® claimed that they had. I called customer support, but was greeted with a "due to unusually high call demand" message that suggested that I use their Web site to solve my problem. Unfortunately, the Web page led me to a dead-end for my type of problem, so I went back to the phones. *Five days later*, I finally got through to a nice lady who apologized profusely, gave me my money back, and generously offered 20 percent off of my next order for my inconvenience.

The call left me feeling unsatisfied. And that's when I decided to do something about it. Under the old economics of influence, I'd be forced to use traditional media channels such as the U.S. Postal Service to express my displeasure. However, as a card-carrying member of the new economics of influence—being a blogger and a podcaster with an audience with whom I could share stories—I opted to produce a seven-minute, lighthearted video called "How 1-800-Flowers Ruined My Life." I posted the video to YouTube on February 24, 2008.[28]

Much to my pleasant surprise, my little video did catch the attention of 1-800-Flowers and, exactly thirty-two days after releasing the video,

---

[28] http://www.youtube.com/watch?v=Wsa7m2KDnEk

on March 28, 2008, I received a polite e-mail from a Jordan Glogau who apologized for any inconvenience and then graciously offered to do something to make it up to me.

Normally, this would have been the end of the story. A customer complains, a company responds, and then everyone goes about the rest of their day. Instead, the plot for this story thickens because Jordan Glogau wasn't the first person to contact me. On February 26, 2008,—just two days after I posted the video—I got the following e-mail from a proprietor of a local florist shop:

> *I just watched your video that you posted. I am sorry to hear about your ordeal with 1-800-Flowers. I hope you know that 1-800-Flowers doesn't represent all florists and to show you what I mean I'll send you a Two Dozen Rose Arrangement from our shop on me. Give me call if you would like,*
>
> *Sincerely, Eric Shaw Owner*
> *Everyday Flowers*
> *www.everydayflowers.net*

I was struck by the juxtaposition of two competitors in the same business—one big, the other small, yet each dealing with the new economics of influence in radically different ways. I decided to dig into the story to learn some more.

New Media as a Better Way to Compete

Everyday Flowers is a local florist shop located in a corporate office park in Tustin, California. Eric Shaw and his wife purchased the shop in 2001 with the hope of building a family-run business together. Like most local florists, Everyday Flowers joined one of the "wire networks," Florists' Transworld Delivery, Inc. (FTD®), for lead generation. FTD promised to bring lots of orders to Everyday Flowers and they completely delivered on that promise. However, even though Everyday Flowers had a steady stream of business coming from FTD, for some reason, Eric just couldn't make ends meet, so he sought the counsel of other florists to see what he was doing wrong.

He began participating in an online forum offered as a courtesy service for FTD affiliates. Eric soon learned that he wasn't alone in his predicament. Spirited discussions between florists nationwide openly considered the possibility that they were somehow suffering from the business that FTD brought them. They discussed how as the wire services (FTD, 1-800-Flowers, Teleflora®, etc.) competed with one another on price, that those florists at the end of the delivery chain were getting squeezed. Just as the conversation got interesting, the FTD-hosted Web site mysteriously disappeared.

No evidence exists that the forums' sponsor pulled the plug in an old economics-of-influence attempt to quell the conversations, but it really doesn't matter. Once conversations begin online they cannot be controlled, as proved through the formation of a new community Web site called *FlowerChat,* which sprang to life to continue the conversation. [29] Since the Web site's founding, *FlowerChat* has amassed more than 3,800 members.

Eric used the information that he learned from the *FlowerChat* forums to take a closer look at his books. That's when he realized that the margins on his FTD-generated business were razor-thin and getting thinner. The more business Eric took from the wire services, the more vulnerable Everyday Flowers became financially. As a result of this analysis, Eric made a very difficult decision—to cut off a significant revenue flow into his struggling company by severing its relationship with FTD. Once completed, Eric committed Everyday Flowers' future to his own marketing efforts, which included his use of New Media technologies.

Like most artistic works, beautiful flower arrangements take time and skill to assemble. Eric believed that if he could demonstrate the labor and skill involved, that he could articulate a clear difference between ordering from a local shop compared with a canned arrangement from a large corporate Web site. He posted videos of his wife designing floral arrangements. The videos weren't professionally polished productions. Some had music, others didn't. Some used time-lapse techniques, while others contained raw recordings— complete with the hum of industrial grade refrigerators in the background.

Between July 19, 2007, and March 16, 2009, Everyday Flowers posted forty-three videos to its YouTube channel, which have collectively been viewed two hundred nine thousand times! [30] The most popular video, a silent slideshow displaying an assortment of wedding bouquets called "Wedding Bouquet Flowers" has been viewed thirty-five thousand times. Always trying to experiment with his new video channel, Eric recently added a "talking

---

[29] http://flowerchat.com
[30] http://www.youtube.com/everydayflowers

balloon" series, offering ten-second video clips that demonstrate the music or messages that these flower accessory items utter when prompted.

Eric says that Everyday Flowers uses YouTube:

- To show that Everyday Flowers is a "real" florist, with no middleman
- To show off some of Everyday Flowers's arrangements instead of the cookie-cutter ones that the wire services promote
- And lastly, to show potential customers how much care, effort, and skill goes into creating these beautiful arrangements

Eric's innovative marketing shift is working. Today, Everyday Flowers is healthier financially than it was when the bulk of its business came from the wire services.

Oh, and he's also noticed an increase in Talking Balloon sales.

One Way to Respond

The day after I received Jordan Glogau's e-mail, I called and thanked him for reaching out to me. I explained that there wasn't anything 1-800-Flowers could do with regards to the six-week-old transaction; however I did have one request. Would he be willing to share the story behind his e-mail to me?

Jordan explained that Monica Woo, president of 1-800-Flowers's Consumer Floral Brand, found my video and forwarded it to her staff for review. "How 1-800-Flowers Ruined My Life" quickly became the center of a debate, as her team tried to determine whether the video was authentic, or something planted by the competition. Evidently, the "production value" of the video was originally assessed as "too good" to be produced by a consumer, and so 1-800-Flowers looked first to rule out a nasty competitor. It took a some digging, but eventually, 1-800-Flowers found my order, determined that the video was real, and that's when Monica Woo handed the case to her reputation manager, Jordan Glogau.

There is one final thing that Jordan did before contacting me. He performed some online research of his own. He discovered that I was a blogger and a podcaster. He checked out my LinkedIn profile. Jordan knew quite a bit about me before ever reaching out, something that helped create rapport as we spoke on the phone. I was pleased that 1-800-Flowers reached out to me in a very sincere way and was even more impressed that the company never requested that I take my video down. 1-800-Flowers understands the new economics of influence. Others in their industry clearly don't.

Another Way to Respond

During my conversation with Jordan, I was stunned to hear that competitors in the floral business would attack another's reputation. "Do your competitors really do that?" I asked.

"Are you kidding?" he replied. "Have you seen the ProFlowers® video?"

I hadn't, so he told me of another online flower vendor called ProFlowers.[31] ProFlowers prides itself in delivering "flowers fresh from the fields" to the consumer. They promise that by eliminating the middleman, that their flowers "will stay fresh and beautiful for at least a week after they arrive." From the consumer's point of view, it sounds like a great deal, but local florists saw it as an attack on their value in the delivery chain. That's when Pennsylvania-based florist Richard Dudley decided to do something about it.

Richard wasn't new to New Media. As the owner of The Bloomery®,[32] he's been a blogger[33] since August 2005, covering any and all flower-related topics—one of which included the advertising practices of a company that positioned local florists as a speed-bump in the flower-delivery chain. By delivering their flowers direct from the grower, ProFlowers made the case that it had the shortest delivery time—the theory being that the less time the flowers spent in transit, the longer that they'd last once delivered to the consumer.

The theory makes logical sense, but competitors both large and small felt that these advertising claims were misleading—a notion that FTD used as the impetus for a lawsuit filed on August 24, 2005, under the tile "Complaint for Unfair Competition by False Advertising, Deceptive Trade Practices, and Intentional Interference with Prospective Economic Advantage."[34] Specifically, the lawsuit claimed that:

- *Flowers are not shipped "direct from the fields" to the customer as advertised by ProFlowers*
- *Statements by Provide Commerce, Inc. (d/b/a ProFlowers) in its own SEC Filings demonstrate that Proflowers' marketing claims to the public are deceptive*

---

[31] http://proflowers.com
[32] http://thebloomery.com and http://floristblogs.com/blogs/bloomery/default.aspx
[33] http://floristblogs.com/blogs/bloomery/default.aspx
[34] http://www.ftdi.com/pressroom/File-StampedComplaint.pdf

The lawsuit and subsequent counter-lawsuit were settled in August 2006, as explained in a jointly-issued press release:

> *In the settlement, neither party admitted to the allegations contained in the claims brought against each other and no money will be paid by either side. The settlement includes a compromise in which FTD agreed to dismiss a separate trademark action brought against Provide Commerce, and in return Provide Commerce agreed to make certain modifications to future advertising. The parties also mutually agreed to abide by certain other guidelines in their advertising after December 31, 2006.*

As FTD and ProFlowers duked it out over advertising practices, local florists grumbled about being portrayed as an extra step between the grower and the consumer. That's when Richard Dudley and his wife, Kathy, decided to do something about it. According to Dudley, a local florist can deliver flowers "off the stem" in the same amount of time as ProFlowers claims—with a significant advantage. Local florists have complete control over the storage environment, something that ProFlowers can't claim with the final delivery stage being put into the hands of third-party transportation services such as the United Parcel Service® or Federal Express®.

The Dudleys decided to demonstrate the consumer's experience by recording an "unboxing." In February 2006, they ordered a dozen assorted roses from ProFlowers.com. Using the primitive video capabilities of a cheap point-and-click camera with a memory card that only held sixty seconds worth of video, the Dudley's only had one chance to record it.

The video opens with Kathy taking an attractive green box with "ProFlowers.com" printed on its side to what appears to be the family's dining room table.[35] She opens the box, first revealing an empty vase followed by something that is expertly wrapped in brown paper. As the paper is removed, we see the long rose stems with their buds closed. So far, everything seems in order, except for a slight rigidity that appears in the stems. That's when Kathy, holding one of the stems like a timpani mallet, gently taps the closed rosebud onto the dining room table. The sound of rosebud on wood reveals that the flowers are frozen solid!

---

[35] Here is the link to the ProFlowers unboxing. http://www.youtube.com/watch?v=FNYGZHPKQgs, but it has since been taken down sometime between June and August.

The video ends with Kathy's unsuccessful attempt to arrange the frozen flowers in the enclosed vase, proving that even the best-trained hands can't do much with twelve rigid stems supporting twelve frozen buds. Through the use of video, the Dudley's had proven their point—without the ability to control the shipping environment, such as a box of roses sitting in a non-environmentally-controlled delivery truck driving through freezing weather—the customer experience would be negatively impacted.

When he published the video to YouTube, Richard hoped that it would get two hundred views. By the spring of 2008, its thirty-one thousand views exceeded his expectations. So how did ProFlowers respond to this video? Did they contact the Dudleys to see if there was anything they could do? No, just as the RBOCs tried controlling their online messaging by purchasing domains ending in "sucks," ProFlowers took a page from the old economics of influence and sent the Dudleys a cease-and-desist letter in May 2008, claiming trademark violations. According to Dudley, the use of "ProFlowers" in the anchor text (links back to the ProFlowers Web site) in the YouTube comments section was considered a trademark violation.[36] Rather than risking costly litigation, the Dudleys decided that it wasn't worth the fight and removed both the YouTube video and its associated blog post.

The Only Thing You Control Is How You React

In the past, it was easy to control your company's brand. You bought advertising. You pitched stories to editors who assigned your stories to their journalists. Today's environment looks totally different. An unhappy customer can write a blog post, a competitor can record an unboxing, and within a few minutes of its posting, anyone in the world can consume and share that content with their friends—for free.

Today, your company has no control over its brand, so what are you going to do about it? Jordan from 1-800-Flowers was the first to admit that, although his company hadn't figured it out yet, he felt that they were on the right track. His mission is to "do the right thing." What's the route your company is going to take?

This story illustrates New Media lessons that every company must heed:

---

[36] ProFlowers never responded to a call to hear their side of the story.

- **Online conversations cannot be stopped**. They can be interrupted for a short while, especially if you control the medium, however, in the age of New Media, where the cost of hosting is negligible and the cost of online user forums software is free, the barrier to online conversation entry is nonexistent.
- **Video is a powerful tool**. With a cheap digital video camera and access to the Web, your business can create and distribute video that distinguishes you from your competition. For free! Also remember that the converse is also true for your competitors.
- **Listen**. Using tools such as Google Alerts, Google News Search, and Google Blog Search will help you discover what's being said about your company. Identify the conversations and respond accordingly.
- **Don't underestimate the creativity of your competition**. New Media has opened up many avenues for storytellers. These storytellers may be competitors or clients, but either way, they are no longer limited by old economics of influence distribution channels. Modern storytellers are only limited by their creativity—which is something that businesses cannot afford to underestimate.

New Media Tip: Engage with your customers, online, offline, or just standing in line.

The Read/Write nature of New Media channels removes the control your company once had over its brand. The only thing left is influence. Engage with your customers. Listen to what they publish about themselves online. Check out their Facebook and LinkedIn profiles. Read their blogs. Watch their online videos. Then, just as 1-800-Flowers reached out to me, reach out to the community that uses your products and services—preferably without the use of a cease-and-desist letter.

Chapter Summary:

- It's not what you say about your company—it's what Google says about it.
- There is no such thing as brand control anymore—there is only brand influence.

- Consumers have access to the same communications technologies as companies. Therefore, they can now talk about brands to a worldwide audience, and there is nothing that companies can do to stop it.
- User-generated content has positive as well as negative repercussions for companies.
- New Media can level the playing field between large and small companies.

Chapter Five

Trust and Faith

A person who trusts no one can't be trusted.

—*Jerome Blattner*

Throughout history, two fundamental truths have prevailed: innovation always disrupts those in power and those at the top don't relinquish power willingly. Innovation ultimately pits two groups of people against one another: those who follow the rules and those who break them. Since New Media technologies smash traditional rules of marketing and public relations, they're frequently the cause of an adversarial relationship between those who prefer change and those who prefer the status quo. As an executive who is looking to bring New Media technologies into your organization, it's important for you to understand that the deck is stacked in favor of the status-quo. As the old adage goes: "Nobody ever got fired for buying IBM."

New Media Tip: Prepare for a long and tiring battle

Those who break the rules of traditional marketing are doomed to a lifelong battle with those who are sworn to protect them.

In 1959, a group of advertising execs from Young and Rubicam® (Y&R) visited a thirty-something radio and recording artist named Stan Freberg. They had a problem with one of their clients, Kaiser® Aluminum Foil, and figured that the young satirist could help them. The group explained that Kaiser only had 5 percent market share in the competitive aluminum foil marketplace, and even more problematic, it lacked distribution channels. The team explained that by the time the local grocers had stocked their shelves with aluminum foil from the dominant leader, Reynolds Wrap®, and the distant second, Alcoa®, there was no room left for Kaiser.

Y&R didn't approach Freberg for his expertise in selling thinly rolled metals. Instead, he was sought for his rule-breaking tendencies—earned while single-handedly turning Madison Avenue upside down with his outlandish idea that commercials could actually entertain people instead of just assaulting them with over-the-top claims. Although the idea was ridiculed by the advertising establishment of the day, anyone who has ever sat through Super Bowl® commercials understands that Stan Freberg was way ahead of his time.

Freberg decided to solve the Kaiser problem by creating a series of commercials that encouraged customers to demand that local grocers carry Kaiser foil. The commercials revolved around a hard luck Kaiser Aluminum Foil salesman named Clark, who battled day after day with grocers who refused to create shelf space for his foil.

Here's an example from one of these commercials:

The scene opens with Clark coming home after a hard day's work. Soap opera music plays in the background as he explains to his wife how bad his day was. From the script:

> **WIFE:** *(SOBBING) Then this means I won't be able to have my operation!*
> One of Clark's children overhears the conversation and interjects:
> **CHILD:** *(IN A SMALL WISTFUL VOICE) Did you bring me some new shoesies, Daddy?*
> **CLARK:** *Ummm … Daddy doesn't have any money for shoesies these days … because the mean old grocers won't stock Daddy's foil.*[37]

When Freberg pitched the script to Y&R, a few chuckles were punctuated by an eruption of fireworks. Some of the rule-followers were concerned that local grocers would be so offended that they'd retaliate by banning Kaiser foil from their stores. Others had a hard time contemplating a commercial

---

[37] It Only Hurts When I Laugh, pg. 159

that willingly branded Kaiser as an underdog. However, the biggest hurdle came in the form of an academic question.

One of the Y&R executives asked, "You didn't go to the Harvard Business School, did you?"[38]

Freberg hadn't.

"Well, I was sure of *that*," he snorted. "If you *had*, they would have taught you one of the primary rules of marketing: Advertising cannot force distribution."[39]

History always repeats itself. There was a time when we knew with certainty that the world was flat and that the sun revolved around the earth. There was a time when we knew, without a doubt, that it was okay for one human being to own another human being. Whereas today, marketers believe that their job is to control both the brand and the message, in 1959, the conventional wisdom held that advertising couldn't force distribution.

The innovator won the argument.

Freberg was given permission to proceed and the Kaiser ad campaign proved to be a complete success. Not only did Kaiser add forty-three thousand new outlets to its distribution channels, but Harvard Business School was forced to revise its curriculum.

Today we face the same problem innovating through New Media. Because of the new economics of influence, communications professionals are forced to question fundamental assumptions that have served them well since the invention of the printing press. Just as Harvard Business School learned that advertising *can* drive distribution, professional communicators need to learn to believe that nonaccredited sources can create reliable content. The remainder of this chapter is dedicated to dealing with the first of these fundamental assumptions: the issue of trust.

Control-to-Influence: The Winners and Losers

The stiffest resistance to New Media innovation comes from those who perceive it as a threat. No matter which departments these employees reside in, whether marketing or public relations, they've spent their entire careers creating, disseminating, and controlling corporate content. The system is

---

[38] It Only Hurts When I Laugh, pg. 162
[39] ibid

tried and true. There is no doubting that it *worked*—past tense being the main distinction.

However, there's a flaw in the system. Advertising vendors who served marketing departments so well in the past are losing their audiences as once-faithful eyeballs turn to younger and more attractive online alternatives. Since advertising costs are traditionally based on cost-per-thousand impressions (CPM), and there are fewer eyeballs to charge for, advertisers are being forced to do one of two things: lower their rates or convince customers to pay the same rates for fewer impressions. Either way, traditional print and broadcast industries are watching their margins erode: forcing them to make cost-cutting decisions that are chronicled daily in blogs such as Paul Gillin's Newspaper Death Watch.[40]

Who is responsible for these wandering eyeballs? Who are these publications losing their audiences to? Today's Stan Frebergs: independent content creators who write blogs, record podcasts, and produce online video. And for the first time in the history of communications, the big dogs of publishing find themselves truly competing with people who love producing content so much that they're willing to do it for free.

Armed with New Media tools, these competitors can do something that the big dogs can't—tell the stories that they want to tell, in their own voice, without having to sell the idea to a grumpy old editor. Traditional media is competing with modern Frebergs who refuse to play the publishing game by the same old set of rules.

At first, the "professionals" ignored the "amateurs," believing that the wandering eyeballs would return to their higher quality of content. Since the New Frebergs didn't follow the rules of journalism, the pros expected them to implode.

The professionals are still waiting.

Some of the most popular blogs now boast audiences that outstrip the readership of major newspapers. A tech news site called TechCrunch has a readership larger than that of the *Los Angeles Times*.[41] That's problematic for two competitive reasons. Not only can TechCrunch deliver its stories at the *speed of bits*, the cost to deliver those bits is independent of the number of subscribers. Newspapers, on the other hand, deliver their content physically on paper and ink. Printed newspapers require delivery people, trucks, fuel,

---

[40] http://www.newspaperdeathwatch.com/
[41] http://techcrunch.com

and time. No matter how many ways you cut it, even if the *Los Angeles Times* perfects the Star Trek teleporter, paper and ink will remain more expensive to deliver than bits.

The professional content creators who once ruled the roost are experiencing a sense of loss and, as a result, they're blaming the newcomers. Traditional media creators look at New Media creators as the Beverly Hillbillies of content creation—people who've gotten their status not through paying their dues, but because they accidentally found oil in their backyard. And so they demonize this new blood, using derogatory terms to describe their efforts, such as "amateur" or "user-generated."

In a recent offsite meeting for a Fortune 50 company, I sat on a panel with podcaster Eric Schwartzman[42] and blogger Steven Timble.[43] Our audience consisted of the company's public relations professionals who opened up a discussion about bloggers versus journalists. For the first fifteen minutes, the differences between journalists and "just a blogger" dominated the conversation. The term, uttered in a derogatory tone, reminded me of the damned-if-you-do-damned-if-you-don't trick question, "So, Senator, do you still beat your wife?"

At about the fifteen-minute mark, I couldn't take it anymore and interrupted the discussion with my own question.

"What do you mean 'just a blogger'?" I asked.

My inquiry caused a pall to pass over the audience. The PR professionals in front of me shot knowing glances to each other before diving straight into the Traditional's Handbook (See Chapter 6) and offering "journalistic integrity," "writing sans opinion," "verifying sources," "editorial control," etc.

Coaches help their players get better. They offer third-party perspectives, help identify bad habits, and offer activities to help eliminate those habits. That's exactly what Eric, Steven, and I attempted to do with these PR professionals. We described the different types of bloggers. We suggested methods for determining the relative importance of a blogger. We offered recommendations for when to engage and when to ignore a blogger. At the end of the meeting, it was clear that our pleading had fallen on deaf ears.

It wasn't the first time that I'd experienced this behavior. I once worked with a very talented director of public relations who spent many a day trying

---

42 http://www.ontherecordpodcast.com
43 http://www.flightglobal.com/blogs/the-dewline/

to convince me that bloggers are evil. Her argument, based more on more fear than facts, frequently ended in a list of disruptions that a rogue blogger could inflict upon her and her job. She spent countless hours worrying about the ramifications that a prickly blog post might cast in her general direction.

Her argument, just as the audience mentioned earlier, centered on the fact that bloggers have no rules to follow, and therefore, their content must be suspect. For her entire career, she had developed a finely tuned process of dealing with the "legitimate press," as she called them, who consisted of journalists who played the corporate news game within well-defined rules. But bloggers, she argued, had no such rules. Bloggers could say anything that they wanted, and that fact alone was enough for her to cast doubt upon every blog and every blog post. Many times I tried to appease her fears, but she'd have none of it.

The good news for her is that journalists are here to stay. The bad news is that there will be far fewer of them for her to interact with. Nevertheless, a silver lining exists. If she's willing to invest the time to build new relationships, she'll find many more avenues for her messages to travel. However, that's the problem.

My PR director friend has spent her entire career playing the old economics-of-influence game. She's built relationships with journalists. She's spent her life building such an efficient mechanism for the dissemination of her public relations messages that she fears having to start all over again, wondering whether or not she has the energy to rebuild her well-honed PR mechanism.

PR professionals must learn new skills to navigate expertly through a content system where the new and the old coexist. This hybrid system will create strange bedfellows as news-only sites compete with news/opinion, which in turn compete with opinion-only sites. New storytellers who write from disparate viewpoints will collectively form a checks-and-balances system for online content. Much to the disappointment of the pros who feel that the consumer will suffer because of hybrid content system, the opposite will occur, as additional sources of content create much more informed consumers.

New Media Is a Faith-Based Initiative

If the new economics of influence create a hybrid form of content creation, how are we—as the content consumers—going to know whom to trust? Journalists claim that we need to trust them because they present unbiased and verified facts. However, knowledge is more than the simple recitation of balanced facts. At The Marketing Profs Digital Marketing Mixer Conference in October 2008, Arianna Huffington of the *Huffington Post* said, "You can't find the truth by covering both sides of an argument and splitting the difference." Independent of what you think of her politics, she's right. A dispassionate view of the facts doesn't necessarily uncover the truth. There must be something else involved—and that something involves trust.

In his book, *The Media Lab*, Stewart Brand describes people's relationships with the information that they consume by pointing out something that is counterintuitive: that people have never paid for the *quality* of the information that they receive. Instead, they pay for the *source* of it. They subscribe to trusted sources of information with the anticipation that quality will come. Some people trust the *New York Times* while others trust the *Wall Street Journal*®. Some trust *Time*® magazine while others trust *Business Week*®. Some trust CNN®, while others trust Fox® News—all independent of the quality of the specific news stories that these news vehicles produce. That's why it's important to take a deeper look at trust. In this new, hybrid-content environment, trust in your sources will prove more important than ever.

A proper discussion on trust isn't complete until we address the fact that new and old media aren't our only trusted sources of information. Daily, we engage with trusted sources that fall outside of traditional media channels. We make decisions, large and small, through polling friends, family, accountants, doctors, lawyers, pastors, and neighbors for their opinions. We want to know if that detergent really makes our shirts whiter; if that paper towel really is the *Quicker Picker-Upper*; or if you think that sportscaster made a racist remark during last night's Monday Night Football game.

In the past, access to this type of information was limited by our physical proximity to the sources. Word-of-mouth only worked when someone was close enough to be heard and likewise, anyone out of earshot was excluded from the discussion. This environment resulted in an advantage for old media, because they could cast information and opinion the farthest.

With New Media, Uncle Jim can blog about the bribe that he was offered at the local town meeting. Cousin Tina can use YouTube to show how a contractor failed to complete her roofing project, causing water damage in her living room. And some guy in Southern California can tell the story of how 1-800-Flowers ruined his life. No longer limited by proximity—fact, opinion, truth, lies, exaggerations, fiction, and entertainment can be created and distributed around the world by the same trusted sources that have helped us make decisions all along. Add social networking sites such as LinkedIn or Facebook, and we can share our trusted sources, as I recommend my advisors and you recommend yours.

In 2001, PR Agency Edelman began its annual Trust Barometer, which asks nearly two thousand people about the level of trust they have in various sources of information such as institutions and companies.[44] In 2006, rather than listing people in leadership positions such as CEOs, managers, journalists, or elected officials, the survey revealed that our most trusted person is "people like me."

When it comes to trust, we as humans gravitate to the people that we identify with. We like talking with people who share our beliefs, drink the same beer, or root for the same football team. In the past, we'd have to schedule our physical lives around connecting with these trusted sources. Today, using New Media technologies, they're only a mouse-click away.

New Content Producers—"People Like Me"

Who do you trust? Do you trust your family? Your spouse? How about your boss or the company that you work for? Do you trust your customers? How about your sources of information? Do you trust the information in a marketing brochure? A banner ad? A direct marketing campaign? Be honest. If your life depended on it, could you really trust the information presented in one of your company's press releases?

Once you see the world through the lens of trust, you start to see the value of New Media channels. Trust is the lubricant of viral message transmission. If marketing's job is to deliver messages to the marketplace, then trust carries those messages the farthest. Alas, traditional marketing has never been built on trust. It has always been built on control.

---

[44] http://www.edelman.com/trust/

Trust Goes Both Ways

Many of my blog posts at ronamok.com come from my battles with corporate employees who are so set in their ways that they refuse to understand New Media. These folks go home at night, praying that this New Media fad will be over so that they can just go back to writing their same old copy, return to their tired old trade shows, and launching their same old specious marketing campaigns. It took me some time, but I finally uncovered a common thread between these individuals. It is the other side of trust.

In 2007 and 2008, as the New Media Evangelist for Synopsys, Inc., I trained more than seventy employees in the art of New Media. "Ken" attended my first class; "Kathy" attended my second; and "Jane" attended my third. Ken and Kathy lit a fire under their New Media activities. Jane took every opportunity that she could to throw cold water on it. Ken and Kathy have incorporated New Media into their worlds. Jane has not only successfully avoided it, but she's convinced others to do the same.

What is it about these first two people that separate them from the third? Why do some people "get it" and others refuse to try? Why do some people see the power of these new communication devices, while others fight them with every fiber of their being? The answer hit me on a nonstop flight from San Jose to Orange County, California. After getting to know Ken and Kathy over that year and a half span, I learned that they both share a similar trait—they trust people. Jane doesn't trust anyone.

New Media requires the ability to make connections with people and making connections with people requires trust. Those who are trustful by nature make for New Media coverts. Those who don't, struggle with the concept. They don't trust what *others* say about *their* products. They don't trust that a customer can arrive at a *correct* purchasing decision without reading the carefully crafted messages that *they* spent weeks working on. Lack of trust drives the "Janes" of the world to seek control of everything.

New Media Tip: Test your company's mettle

Who does your company trust? The answer to this question will help determine its ability to adopt and use New Media effectively.

Be Careful. We Can See You

New Media channels are based on trust and therefore most of them are designed to be open. For example, Wikipedia allows anyone to edit its pages, which sometimes tempts old-school marketers into playing shenanigans with them. The problem with this practice is that every edit entered into Wikipedia is logged and the results are publicly available. Unknown to most Wikipedia users, this fact has resulted in embarrassing situations for those who've tried to hide their actions behind perceived anonymity.

As an executive, it's important for you to understand that the online activities of your employees while logged into your networks, whether physically at the office or through a VPN connection from home, can create potential embarrassments for your company. Such an example happened while I was at Synopsys, when we discovered that an unknown employee was performing stealthy operations under the perceived veil of anonymity. Here's the story.

The world of electronics is self-governed by industry standards: written agreements between competitors to build components such that they play nice with one another. For example, "USB" is an industry standard that stands for Universal Serial Bus. USB is a specification that all electronic manufactures agree to build compliant devices against. It doesn't matter whether a customer connects a flash drive, digital camera, or an iPod into a USB; as long as each manufacturer built the devices to the USB specification, they should all "plug and play" together.

Industry standards are for the betterment of the industry as a whole because each manufacturer can create products that serve the needs of the common customers. Before an industry standard is created however, the politics can get pretty heated. Sometimes competing standards backed by fierce competitors can slow the entire process down, as each is so heavily invested in their own version of the standard that they refuse to budge. An example is the debate between Common Power Format[®45] (CPF)—backed by

---

[45] http://en.wikipedia.org/wiki/Common_Power_Format

a company called Cadence Design Systems®, and the Unified Power Format® (UPF)—backed by its archrival, Synopsys.

On February 17, 2007, at precisely 12:28 a.m., someone edited Cadence's Common Power Format (CPF) Wikipedia page, adding the following sentence to the descriptive intro: *Thousands have died in the creation of this wretched format. And thus the industry has moved on.*[46]

The vandalism didn't stop there. At 10:03 p.m. on the same day, another vandal changed the name of the format from "*Common Power* Format" to "*Cadence Proprietary* Format."

A closer inspection of the edits shows that the "thousands have died" vandal arrived at Wikipedia through an IP address of 198.182.56.5. The number looks harmless enough until it's run through a free online service called Whois.net, which revealed that IP address 198.182.56.5 belongs to Synopsys, Inc. located at 700 E. Middlefield Road, Mountain View, CA. In a nutshell, someone from Synopsys's corporate headquarters sabotaged the Wikipedia entry for a competitor's proposed standard.

The revelation was a sobering experience because Synopsys didn't sanction this activity. It was likely the work of a rogue employee who probably thought that it was cute. Unfortunately events like this can give your company an embarrassing black eye, which will live online, archived forever.

IP addresses can be tracked and your company will be guilty by association with the activities performed by employees using your network. Consider using this story as Synopsys did to teach employees about the dos and don'ts of New Media. The first thing that the company did was update its Social Media Policy. Next it wrote an article for the company's internal employee Web site that essentially said, "Don't do that!"

New Media Tip: Seek transparency

Be transparent in everything you do online or be prepared to suffer the consequences.

---

[46] http://en.wikipedia.org/w/index.php?title=Common_Power_Format&action=history

Chapter Summary:

- Old communications rules don't work with new media channels.
- New content creators are challenging the rules of traditional content creators such as journalists and marketing and public relations professionals.
- Trust through transparency is the most important aspect of online content.

Chapter Six

The Traditional's Handbook

○ ○

If I still believe something after five years, I doubt it.

—Marvin Minsky

Everyone has an opinion about New Media. Some are informed, others aren't, and most fall somewhere in between. Employees who are set in their ways will resist change, while others are willing to change everything. Adopting New Media sparks such diverse opinions that it's important for executives to have tools by which to calibrate them. This chapter identifies New Media challenges and gives you a prism through which to filter them.

Be Careful Whom You Ask

We have a love-hate relationship with "new." Although most love getting a new car, a new house, or a new cell phone, if changes result, especially in our daily routines, resistance is natural. The biggest obstacle that executives face when trying to fit New Media channels into their businesses comes in the form of inertia.

As a New Media evangelist, I've seen hundreds of different reactions to the concept of adding New Media channels to organizations. Over the years, I've been able to categorize those reactions into three different personality types: The "Get-Its," the "Traditionals," and my favorite group, those "Running with Scissors." A solid understanding of the three personality types will help executives make the best decisions.

It takes less than thirty seconds to determine which category someone falls into. Some people lean forward in their chairs and listen intently as they envision New Media ways to solve problems that have plagued them for years. Others will lean back in their chairs, arms crossed, working themselves into a defensive mindset.

Clients are usually surprised to hear that my three categories have nothing to do with age, assuming incorrectly that younger people naturally adopt New Media quicker than older folks. Although younger folks are less resistant to change than older folks are, age isn't the determining factor. Instead it comes down to a fundamental question:

Are they willing to relinquish control in favor of influence?

The "Get-Its"

Get-Its are people who latch onto the new economics of influence immediately. They're typically not afraid of adopting new ways of doing things, nor do they have adverse reactions to change. *Get-Its* are willing to try new things; to experiment. They understand the principles of transparency and are willing to learn more about incorporating them into their communications.

Though *Get-Its* are open to New Media concepts, they aren't necessarily Pollyannas about them. Members of this group carry a healthy dose of skepticism in their questions. They plan before jumping in, simultaneously understanding that some answers may not be immediately available. *Get-Its* understand that New Media is exactly that, "new," and therefore they balance planning and exploring. *Get-Its* will provide the best information with which to make your decisions, because they'll present a balanced view of why certain technologies fit within your organization and why others don't.

The "Running with Scissors"

Running-with-Scissors are people who "get it," but in a dangerous way. They're the employees who dive into the pool without checking where the deep end is. They're enthusiastic about trying anything new, and are so excited about playing with new tools, technologies, and methods, that they'll run haphazardly throughout an organization with them. And just as their name suggests, they represent the most likely group to blacken a corporate eye with New Media.

Of the three types, *Running-with-Scissors* require the largest investment of executives' time. Managers must balance their employees' exuberance for new technology with the business goals of the company, reining in corporate risk without choking raw enthusiasm. *Running-with-Scissors* employees possess essential skills for the successful adoption of New Media—specifically the initiative to work with new and buggy software and the stamina to overcome inherent limitations. Appropriate leadership harnesses this valuable group of employees for your New Media team.

The Traditionals

If the *Get-Its* are the easiest group to manage and the *Running-with-Scissors* are the most time-consuming, then the *Traditionals* are by far the most difficult. *Traditionals* not only don't "get it," but they are adamant about "not getting it."

Traditionals are probably your most productive employees. They are extremely competent in their jobs, which is precisely the reason they resist change. *Traditionals* quickly understand the disruptions that New Media technologies introduce into their carefully organized worlds. Hence, *Traditionals* tend to see New Media as a threat to their jobs, and they'll do everything within their power to stop it.

I encountered my first *Traditional* in the mid-90s. The Internet was just becoming popular and companies were making tough decisions about their Web sites. One such decision involved the display capabilities of most computer monitors. Even though graphic designers had a palate of millions to choose from, most computers displayed only 256 colors. When designers created pages using more than 256 colors, the graphics cards substituted existing colors for those that were missing, resulting in hideously mismatched, often illegible Web pages. *Traditionals* were so focused on perfect color selection that they saw the Web as useless. My first *Traditional* tried to convince me that the Web would hurt her brand. "You can't market effectively using less than 256 colors!" she said.

As an executive, you must set the bar within your organization. It's up to you to put together an interdisciplinary team that can handle all of the issues surrounding the adoption of New Media within your organization. The *Get-Its* are required for their thoughtfulness and generally positive outlook. The *Running-with-Scissors* are required for their enthusiasm, which will be needed within the organization when things don't work out as planned. Although it is crucial for *Traditionals* to participate because of their vast knowledge, as the senior member of the New Media group, your job is to address their concerns while preventing them from derailing the project.

Make it Go Away

I'm guessing that she was one of the three people left in the world who had never seen a YouTube video. Unfortunately, her company had chosen to join the ranks of Ford®, Intel®, and Sun® Microsystems, which also used YouTube as a video-hosting service.

Her group had produced a three-minute video, and so she followed the tried-and-true procedure for getting a Web page built. Within a very short amount of time, her Web team had designed a page, uploaded the video to YouTube, and embedded that video within it.

As she had always done, she went through the new page with a fine-toothed comb. She checked every word for accuracy and spelling. She made sure the correct messaging was there. And then, she played the video.

Her report summarized her findings and explained that everything looked good—except for the end of the video, which acted strangely. Rather than ending where it should, two undesirable things popped onto her screen: a menu of unrelated videos followed by some YouTube-embedded code stuff.

As a *Traditional*, used to 100 percent control over her content, she delivered her ruling: "Make it go away," she said.

I have to admit that I chuckled when I saw her message. I'm forced to deal with these things all of the time. And to be fair, I really shouldn't have laughed, because she just didn't understand. All she wanted was for things to remain the same—with her controlling 100 percent of her content—something that disappeared with the birth of RSS-driven technologies such as blogs, podcasts, and wikis.

I tried to explain that what she saw was normal. "Every YouTube video acts the same way," I said. "People expect it. It's good. It's all good."

But "good" wasn't the way she saw it. And so she fought with me. Instead of hearing my case, she went off to disprove my "facts" by finding "other" companies that were not only using "YouTube," but had figured out how to eliminate the funky endings, too.

Of course, none of her examples used YouTube—they were either self-hosted (something her IT department had already prohibited) or were paying third-party video hosting providers.

I tried one last time. I explained that soon, when her company had published many videos on YouTube, that in all likelihood, those videos would come up as suggestions. My advice fell on deaf ears. Words like "probable," "likelihood," and "trust," don't sit very well with those expecting control, and she responded by killing the entire project. I protested, but she'd have none of it. If she couldn't retain complete control over every aspect of the video, then she'd take her ball and go home.

The Traditional's Handbook

A time will come when your New Media team consisting of *Get-its*, *Running-with Scissors*, and *Traditionals* will be assembled. The *Get-Its* will come to the meeting prepared with project ideas, both pro and con, for discussion. *The Running-with-Scissors* folks will offer their enthusiastic support. The *Traditionals* will be there for one reason only, to maintain the status quo. For support, they'll dig deeply into the *Traditional's* Handbook, a collection of objections designed to halt change. The rest of this chapter will take a look at their most common objections, so that you can be prepared for them.

What's the ROI?

The $64,000 question that all *Traditionals* ask when feeling the pinch of New Media is:

"Okay. What's the Return on Investment?"

It's a fair question. There should be some way to track measurable business benefits of an investment in New Media, so let's give it a try:

- If your company spends $10,000 to make $11,000, then it has a return on investment of 10 percent.
- Or, if your company invests $100,000 into new software that saves $40,000 per year, that investment will pay for itself in two and a half years.

Profit is a two-variable equation. So, if your company can increase revenues or reduce costs, then it enjoys a positive ROI.

But what happens if your company invests $0 and still gets some sort of benefit from it? How do we then calculate ROI? To put it another way, how does one divide by zero?

For example:

- Your company can download Wordpress and have a blog up and running on its own site—at no cost.
- Employees can use their personal hand-held digital cameras to record video demonstrations of your flagship products, upload those videos to YouTube, and pay nothing for every customer who sees it.
- A member of your marketing team can build a fan page on Facebook, connect with colleagues, get introduced to prospects, and get answers from trusted resources—for free.
- Your employees can microblog on Twitter, breaking industry news, pointing customers to relevant information, or providing expertise to those who seek it—again for free.
- Your company can take digital photographs at a trade show, load them onto Flickr, and share them with your favorite customers— for, guess what? Free.
- And you can use RSS to stay informed about your industry, your customers, and your competitors—you get the point.

In these scenarios, with *any* increase in revenues or reduction in costs—whether product sales, qualified prospects, or branding—the ROI is *infinite*.

New Media may not require money, but it does require time and talent. They are corporate resources that executives must manage. Therefore, since New Media technologies offer such high (divide by zero) leverage, managers must at least consider if a small investment of their employees' time is worth the potential return on it. The upside is just too high to ignore.

Take the case of the corporate blogger who wrote for one of my clients. He posted once every other week, spending an average of two hours per post. After about six months, he'd built a modest audience of about three hundred RSS subscribers.

Now let's assume that the fully burdened cost of his position (salary, training, benefits, office, and computer) was $200,000 per year. Rounding that number to $100 per hour (for a forty-hour week), his employer spent $200 for each post that he wrote. Put another way, the company paid $200 for every message he delivered to his three hundred existing subscribers.

Remember, a blog isn't a one-shot deal like a marketing campaign, tradeshow booth, or corporate newsletter. A blog creates a growing repository of relevant content—a searchable database for both present and *future* readers. Today our blogger has more than six hundred RSS subscribers, which drops his cost per subscriber from $0.66 originally to $0.33 today.

That's the investment. Now let's look at possible returns. While gaining readers, our corporate blogger is:

- establishing trust with a growing audience;
- becoming a respected expert in his field; and
- creating a sought-after resource.

Given these facts, what is the ROI when he:
- speaks at a major industry conference?
- accompanies your business development folks on a sales call?
- spurs a customer to contact your company directly?
- instantly quells fear, uncertainty, and doubt (FUD) that your competitor is spreading about your company?

New Media Tip: Divide by zero

Run the numbers for yourself. Are divide-by-zero *returns* worth prioritizing an *investment* of one hour per week? Are they worth 1/40th of your employee's fully burdened cost?

Marketing and PR have always provided soft numbers with regards to ROI. PR measures the number of times a story has been picked up from a press release. Advertising tracks how many "impressions" a banner ad generated. Marketing determines how many page views a campaign created. All are acceptable business measurements. We haven't spent enough time with New Media to determine what the acceptable measurements are yet, but let's be very clear: New Media is by far the most measurable content distribution platform that exists today.

We'll take a closer look at specific New Media measurements in Chapter 10.

Who has time to do this stuff?

New Media technologies throw a new wrinkle into the decision process—the fact that adoption requires an investment of more time than money. Good managers guard their staff's time, so when approached by someone to supply bloggers, a manager is likely to say, "My employees are already too busy doing their "real" jobs. Where are they gonna find time to become bloggers?"

It's easy to assume that corporate blogging is a full-time job. It isn't, but it does require some time, and management must determine the amount acceptable for a return on its investment. Karen Bartleson of Synopsys releases blog posts every Thursday. It takes her about an hour to write each post. She has eighteen hundred RSS subscribers. Would you support her investment of time?

Nobody reads blogs

Very early into a discussion about corporate blogging, it's common for a *Traditional* to say something such as, "I don't know why people are getting so excited about this stuff. I've seen the research. Most blogs don't get much readership."

There's nothing factually incorrect about this observation. It's true; most blogs don't get the readership of the *New York Times*. But that's the point. Corporate blogs are designed to attract the *right* audience not a *big* audience. The inefficiencies of the old economics of influence required large audiences to make the probabilities work out. The new economics of influence relies on the power of small numbers. Instead of trying to put a blog before as many eyeballs as possible in hopes that people will read it, blogging is about producing specialized content that attracts the *right* audiences. Blogging is about audiences that self-select your content instead of self-ignoring it (think TiVo®). *Traditionals* demanding tens of thousands of impressions won't be impressed with a corporate blog that has attracted an audience of two hundred RSS subscribers because comparatively speaking, it looks like a failure. But without understanding what an RSS subscriber actually represents, companies may inadvertently cast aside their most important customers and prospects.

By going out of her way to subscribe to your corporate blog via RSS, a subscriber made a choice. She's telling you that not only does she like your content, but she likes it so much that she's willing to open up a special content channel for you—something that's not to be taken lightly because she has given you things that are hard to achieve. She's given you her time and her trust. She trusts that your content will maintain the quality that she sampled before subscribing. She trusts that you'll release new content with the same frequency.

Don't try to compare the large audiences of the old economics of influence with the small audiences of the new economics of influence. To do so is to totally miss the point.

New Media Tip: Seek the power of the tiny audience

Which is more important? Ten thousand looky-loos driven to your Web site by a contest to win an iPhone or two hundred RSS subscribers who are passionate about your products or services? There's power in the tiny audience. It's the power of influence.

New Media isn't professional

Professional business communicators have been trained to write in corporate, first-person plural voice. The conversational style of New Media content is typically written in first-person singular, which some consider unprofessional. But what is professional? Isn't professionalism determined by success? Both styles of writing are appropriate, but is one better than the other? Put them side by side and ask yourself the following question:

After my customers consume each form of content, are they closer to buying my products or services?

The more effective form should be considered professional.

New Media Tip: Talk like a human being

Is taking a client to a football game unprofessional? How about a round of golf? When you are at one of these venues with a client, are you speaking in professional corporate-speak or unprofessional human-speak?

Yeah, but has anyone run this by legal yet?

Whatever you want to call the legal department, whether it's the "Department of No" or the "Department of Sales Prevention," we live in a litigious society, and our corporate attorneys are necessary. Although they may appear paranoid, they have good reason. Their job is to assess potential risk. The more risk they perceive, the more nervous they get. I learned early on that if you involve legal in your plans from the very beginning, your legal department can provide excellent advice. The converse is also true. If you create plans without their help and expect them to rubber stamp their approval at the end of the process, they can turn your world into a living hell.

The first thing that you need is a "New Media Policy" that creates clear guidelines for the use of New Media channels. Such a document will kill two birds with one stone, not only giving guidance to employees, but also giving upper management the confidence to support the activities. If you want to create a corporate blogging policy, check out *The Corporate Blogging Handbook*, by Debbie Weil.

I recommend that clients develop a simple policy containing the following sections:

1. Use the Company Handbook
2. Identify Yourself
3. Respect Copyrights
4. Don't Tell Secrets
5. Seek Permission
6. Respect Those in the Community
7. Fix Mistakes First
8. Be an Interesting Expert
9. Fact-Check, Spell-Check, and Check Again

Run the first draft by legal. Let them know what you are trying to do. Show them the New Media policies of other companies such as Sun Microsystems[47] and IBM.[48] Work together until you arrive at an agreed-upon document. Here's a test to see if your document will be effective: if the policy makes *you* feel a tad restricted while *legal* feels a bit exposed, then it's probably perfect.

Once you have the document okayed by legal, you're on your way. For some reason, *Traditionals* are terrified of the legal department, so the next time they question your company's ability to use New Media, drop your

---

[47] http://www.sun.com/communities/guidelines.jsp
[48] http://www.ibm.com/blogs/zz/en/guidelines.html

legal-approved document on their desks. More often than not, they'll stare slack-jawed and capitulate.

Our customers are too old for New Media

In their book, *Wikinomics*, Don Tapscott and Anthony D. Williams call the two billion people born between 1977 and 1997 the "Net-Generation," since they've always had access to computers and the Internet. This group thinks in fundamentally different ways than Baby Boomers or Gen-Xers. They are natural collaborators. They not only believe information should be free; as individuals, they also believe they have the right to remix, mash up, or manipulate the content that they consume. Net-Genners distrust traditional marketing, ignore advertising, and yet are perfectly comfortable receiving and relaying "messaging" through their peers.

Let's do some math. The Net-Genners born in 1977 are now thirty-two. They've been out of high school for fourteen years, and have been out of college for almost ten. Entry-level management starts at about five years, middle management at eight. Therefore, for the next twenty years, two billion Net-Genners will be infiltrating middle management, bringing with them their network-driven belief systems.

Ask your Traditionals this: "Is ignoring two billion potential customers really worth the risk?"

New Media Tip: Think Passionographics not Demographics
Traditional demographic data doesn't account for passion—something that motivates people to participate in social networking sites such as Facebook. Think about categorizing New Media users more by their passions than by their age. For example, the average age of a Harley Davidson owner is forty-seven years old[49]—not typically considered by the Traditionals as within the "New Media demographic." Yet, Harley Davidson's Facebook fan page has over one hundred eighty-five thousand fans! Find where your passionate customers live online, then create content that helps them satisfy their informational cravings.

---

[49] http://investor.harley-davidson.com/demographics.cfm?bmLocale=en_US

Chapter Summary:

- Employees attempting to use New Media can be categorized three ways: "Get-Its," "Running with Scissors," and the "Traditionals."
- Executives must understand the motivations of each group in order to make informed decisions.
- There are many objections to the use of New Media, such as ROI, professionalism, and measurement. All must be understood before using New Media technologies.

Chapter Seven

Business as a Publisher

On the Web, you are what you publish.

—*David Meerman Scott*

New Media Requires New Content

Humans are creatures of habit when it comes to adopting new technologies. Marvin Minsky, the father of artificial intelligence, calls this "the investment principle," a concept explaining why our older ideas have unfair advantage over our newer ones. We only need to look at history to see how bad we are at adapting to communications innovations. For example, television was introduced at the peak of the golden age of radio. Instead of taking full advantage of the fact that television could do things that radio couldn't, such as telling stories using moving pictures, the first television shows simply filmed radio announcers standing in front of microphones! Early television producers executed a lateral translation from one technology to another, figuring myopically that if families enjoyed gathering around radios to listen to their favorite radio dramas, then they'd love watching those performances live. The radio-to-television translation isn't the only example of our habit-bound ways. In the 1990s, the first corporate Web pages were simply product brochures repurposed for online consumption.

Our natural comfort with the familiar feeds our proclivity to performing linear translations from the old to the new. The investment principle, combined with our reluctance to embrace change, keeps us from seeking the sweet spot of any new medium. Whenever I explain the virtues of corporate blogging to clients, it's common for PR managers to say something such as, "Cool, let's put our press releases into a blog!" I can't blame them for this reaction. They're simply doing what their predecessors did, putting radio announcers in front of television cameras. Until companies take advantage of the unique capabilities of new communications media, they'll continue to flounder in their attempts. This chapter will tackle the lesson that every company must learn, that *a new medium deserves new content.*

What Exactly Is Content?

My friend Rick Palmer has always threatened to write a book called "Why Words Don't Work." His premise is that because people interpret words so differently, the meaning of everyday phrases is frequently the source of confusion. That couldn't be truer today than with an important—and perhaps overused—word: content.

If you look up the word in the dictionary, you'll find an overloaded term. For example, there's con*tent*, as in "Are you con*tent* with the font that I'm using in this book?" Or there's the *con*tent of a package, as in "Did the *con*tents of the fruit basket arrive unspoiled?" And lastly, there is *con*tent, as in "The *con*tent on your Web site is about as exciting as watching water boil." We'll focus on the final definition for the rest of the book.

Content is the cornerstone upon which your company must build its online communications strategy. In the information age, the most important thing that your company has to offer is the information it provides online. So, how will this information stand out from the rest? If you placed the online content that your company publishes side-by-side with that of your competitor's—which would your prospects and customers prefer to read?

Web sites in the 1990s worked fairly well under the old economics of influence, when companies tightly controlled their branding messages. However, as more content moves online, you must ask if a static online brochure is the best way to compete within the online marketplace of ideas.

Your corporate Web site represents a place to stake your online claim. It is a platform for you to speak in an unfiltered, straight-from-the-horse's-mouth manner. Whether it be case studies on how customers have benefited from your products or services, or venues for responding to negative news, the corporate Web site is the platform from which to orchestrate the education of the marketplace.

Has your CEO ever been misquoted in the press? Then use your Web site to set the record straight by providing a full transcript of your conversation with the reporter as Mark Cuban does on his blog, Blog Maverick.[50] Do you have a disgruntled customer spreading fear, uncertainty, and doubt (FUD) about your products and services? Instead of dealing with it on a customer-by-customer basis, use your corporate Web site to tell your side of the story. The difference between today's corporate Web sites and the standard 1990s site is its purpose. One praises the company without any benefit to the visitor. The other serves both visitor and company by providing useful information, services, and solutions to customers' problems. You must consider both sides before staking your company's claim in cyberspace.

"Good" Content and "Bad" Content

If New Media channels require new content, then there must be some way to rate it. Is there a nonsubjective way to determine if the content on your Web site is better than someone else's? Is the quality of your content objective or subjective? One company has dedicated itself to this very question. Its goal is to separate the online wheat from the online chaff. Its nineteen thousand employees focus their ingenuity and expertise on this problem as they work to *organize the world's information and make it universally accessible and useful.*[51]

Of course I'm talking about Google, the eight-hundred-pound gorilla of Internet search. Since its founding, Google has developed ways to scour the Internet for information, then rank-order that information from most important/relevant to least important/irrelevant. The better they get at ranking the world's content, the more people use the service, the more advertising they sell, and the more money their stockholders make. The contrary is also true. If Google ends up indexing the world's worst information and portrays it as anything else, people will stop using the search engine, ad revenues will dry up, and the shareholders will not be happy.

Google has built a business on its ability to determine "good" from "bad" content through its proprietary PageRank algorithm. Although the contents of this algorithm are more tightly held than the recipe for Coca-Cola®, it shares some similarities. We may not know the exact proportions,

---

50 http://blogmaverick.com
51 Google's corporate mission: http://www.google.com/intl/en/corporate/

but we do know the list of ingredients, such as caramel color, sugar, caffeine, and so on.

We know that Google favors incoming links, the theory being that if you have a Web page that is valuable enough for others to add a hyperlink to it, then the PageRank algorithm gives it a thumbs-up. The more incoming links your content draws, the higher that page moves up the search rankings. We also know that Google prefers updated content to the stagnant variety. If your company has a 1990s site, the odds are that PageRank algorithm is wondering whether or not you're still minding the store.

In the past, companies paid consultants thousands of dollars for Search Engine Optimization (SEO). And although there are still tips and tricks that SEO consultants can do to "optimize" your search results, by far, the most bang-for-the-SEO-buck is to create fresh content customers find so useful that they refer others to it. If the content that you publish online is created with that mantra, you have the majority of the SEO battle licked. The converse is also true. If you hire a SEO consultant promising a top Google placement while using various "red-saber" techniques to game the system,[52] your site will likely be sacked by Matt Cutts, the head of Google's Webspam team,[53] who'll eventually find out and punish your company for the deception.

Professional communicators are very good at creating content. Unfortunately, what was once considered good content for old media channels is generally bad content for New Media channels. Without modifying how they create content for the online world, professional communicators will follow the same path as their counterparts from the golden age of radio. New Media deserves new content. You can't take a press release, designed for journalists looking for stories, and release it as compelling New Media content.

> *COMPANY NAME, a world leader in SOMETHING THAT CAN'T BE DISPUTED, who makes seamlessly integrated, value-added, NAME OF PRODUCT FAMILY here, has just released SOME WIZZ-BANG NEW OR REDESIGNED*

---

[52] In the *Star Wars*® series, all of the bad guys use red lightsabers™ while the good guys carry other colors. John Wall of *MarketingOverCoffee.com* coined the term "red saber" to refer to the deceptive practices that "black hat" SEO practitioners use to trick search engines.

[53] http://www.mattcutts.com/blog/

PRODUCT. ADD FABICATED QUOTE FROM EXECUTIVE/CLIENT HERE. If you have any questions, contact NAME HERE.

Is the content of a press release so compelling that you'd send it to a friend? Is it so interesting or so valuable that you'd write a blog post about it, including a hyperlink to it? Just for kicks, take a look at your company's Web site right now. What does the content look like? Do you offer content that visitors can't find anywhere else? If you had your own blog, would you truly want to add a hyperlink to any part of your corporate Web site? Yahoo! has a quick way to display the number on inbound links to a site. It's called Site Explorer.[54] Give it a whirl. How many inbound links does it list for your corporate Web site? Lots? If not, the odds are that your company is publishing "bad" content.

New Media Tip: Self online evaluation

One of the most useful free resources on the Web is Hubspot.com's Web site grader.[55] Use it to analyze your Web site and then act on its recommendations.

The Corporate Blog

Search engines such as Google prefer content that is:

- relevant;
- updated periodically; and
- that others consider so valuable that they hyperlink to it.

Put another way: Google loves blogs!

The most cost-effective way for your company to add good content to your site—even if it is currently a 1990s site—is to add an interesting and useful blog to it. By doing so, you will have begun transforming your site from a static brochure to a functional source of relevant content.

A corporate blog is the most influential online publication your business can offer to its customers and prospects. It is a communications vehicle that, if used properly, can provide customer insights that traditional white papers, marketing collateral, or PR can't because it is written in a totally different style.

---

[54] http://siteexplorer.search.yahoo.com/
[55] http://website.grader.com/

Most corporate documents are written in first-person plural, the "royal we" tense, as in "we provide custodial products and services," or "we develop emergency backup systems for data storage." Rarely is the term "I" used in the world of professional business communications. However, a corporate blog uses "I" liberally because posts carry more than a simple collection of dry facts. Blogs are written by real people who share their opinions in conversational and transparent voices. The fact that bloggers share their opinions is by far the largest inhibitor when it comes to convincing professional business communicators that blogging is the right choice for a company.

Conventional wisdom within the professional communications community is that objectivity and credibility are mutually exclusive. They aren't. Can a business-sponsored information source offer an objective viewpoint with respect to their products and services? No, of course not. Neither can a press release. Nobody expects that. Corporate-sponsored information will always be viewed as biased; however, bias isn't the Achilles' heel that critics think it is. Readers of corporate blogs will happily consume biased content as long as the source remains transparent about the fact and the content is interesting or useful. The alternative is far more dangerous.

People despise content sources that claim to be one thing—but turn out to be another. Although Bill Maher and Rush Limbaugh incite strong audience reactions through their openly left and right-leaning opinions, their audiences relish the bias. Former CBS news anchor Dan Rather suffered the wrath of those who felt duped by him reporting news as unbiased when, in fact, it wasn't. That is a lesson that all professional communicators should heed. Be transparent about everything that you do and your readers will reward you for it. Ignore this practice and be ready to accept the consequences because someone will find out. As my good friend Rich Davis says, "People have pretty good B.S. detectors."

New Media Tip: Admit it. You are biased
Admit your bias and people will take your content at face value.

Executives seeking to bring New Media into their companies must be prepared to fight the battle for transparent communications because *Traditionals* have black belts in the art of spin. If there is a bug in your software, they're expected to hide it. If your CEO said something stupid in her most recent keynote address, they must spin it effortlessly. If, on the other hand, your company encourages its bloggers to discuss the good, the bad, and the ugly, make sure to have the company defibrillator handy, as your *Traditionals* and execs may clutch their chests and fall to the floor.

Transparency and credibility are close cousins. No matter what readers believe about the biases of corporate bloggers, by remaining transparent about the relationship, all gain credibility and influence, two very powerful, yet hard to achieve accomplishments in a skeptical world.

Transparency and Credibility

Many years ago, I was an applications engineer for Valid Logic Systems, a company that sold software tools to electrical engineers. An application engineer was an employee with a degree in electrical engineering, who tagged along with a sales rep to help answer technical questions. In the grand scheme of things, a sales team like this forms a "white hat/black hat" alliance, with the sales rep wearing the black hat and the applications engineer, the white. The black-hat asks the tough questions and is always trying to close people. The white-hat demonstrates the product, answers all of the technical questions, and frequently supports customers post-sale.

More often than not, an intriguing dynamic developed between the end-customer and me, the applications engineer. On one hand, we had similar backgrounds. We had successfully navigated our way through engineering school and had been working in the industry designing circuits. On the other hand, we sat on opposite sides of the same table. My job was to help convince the customer to purchase our software. The customer, on the other hand, needed to determine whether our software would perform correctly.

Never for one minute did my prospect think that I was unbiased in my opinion. At the same time, that didn't stop me from establishing credibility as a knowledgeable resource. It is possible to build credibility without objectivity. It is possible to have a biased opinion *and* to also tell the truth. Although these statements fly in the face of conventional wisdom, two people with strong opinions and different agendas can actually arrive at a good decision. It happens every day.

One of the best credibility-building lessons that I learned came from observing a fellow applications engineer demonstrate a software product. I was sitting in the back of a room packed with about twenty people. In the middle of her demo, someone in the audience asked her how the product handled a specific technical issue. Without skipping a beat, she looked at him, shrugged her shoulders, and said, "Not very well," continuing to explain some of the product's shortcomings along with some of the ways our customers worked around the deficiency.

I remember two things about this exchange: the gasp that I let out and the shade of red our sales rep turned. In his eyes, she had trashed our product instead of showing it in the best possible light. What he didn't understand at the time was that she had just established a foundation for her credibility, which manifested itself about ten minutes later when someone asked about another technical capability. This time, she turned, smiled, and enthusiastically described how her product excelled in those areas, rattling off how customers used the feature to solve all sorts of common problems. Her body language showed confidence and pride, and her voice was filled with enthusiasm.

In that instant, she had gained credibility. By being transparent—by admitting that our product still had its warts—she had established herself as a credible source. The engineers in that room knew that if they asked her a question, they'd get a straight answer.

Transparency and credibility carry great distances. Think about the trap that she set for any competitors that demonstrate their products in the future. The next time those prospects witness a demonstration from a competitor and every question is answered with, "It's the greatest thing since sliced bread," who do you think will be considered the more credible source? Both demonstrators are biased, but one is transparent and the other isn't.

Valid Logic Systems got the sale. The competitor didn't.

Encourage your corporate bloggers to be transparent. It won't always be easy, but it will always establish credibility.

Building an Audience through Nanoscoping

Nanoscoping: Choosing such a narrow subject that it increases the probability that a specific audience can find it through online search.

Traditional corporate content created by professional communicators is frequently of the "one-off" variety. Press releases are issued once. Brochures are created to support specific product models. White papers are stand-alone documents created and released independently. But New Media channels such as blogs or podcasts (audio and video) are considered "serial" content sources, which are released at somewhat regular intervals. Just as your favorite sitcom comes on every Monday evening at 8:00 p.m., your favorite blog or podcast should come to you at somewhat regular intervals.

Creating serial content rather than traditional "one-off" marketing content requires you to rethink your strategy before diving into the competitive online landscape. With infinite publishers competing for the fragmented attention spans of finite customers, how does a company stand a chance at finding an audience at all?

There's a scene in *Zen and the Art of Motorcycle Maintenance* that describes a student with writer's block.[56] She wants to write a five-hundred-word essay about the United States, yet her professor suggests that she narrow her topic. Instead of trying to write about an entire nation, he recommends that she write about something more specific—such as her hometown of Bozeman, Montana. She can't do it. So, he asks her to narrow her subject to Main Street in Bozeman. She still can't do it. Frustrated, he says,

"Narrow it down to the front of one building on the main street of Bozeman. The Opera House. Start with the upper left-hand brick."

She returns with a five-thousand-word essay.

Companies that choose to incorporate blogging into their online content offerings should ask their bloggers to choose razor-thin topics. By carving out the narrowest of the narrow, a world of possibility opens, simultaneously making it easier to write for and to attract a passionate audience. If your corporate blog is a source of information that can't be found anyplace else, then you're on the right track.

Take Karen Bartleson from Synopsys, Inc., for example. Karen is an electrical engineer and corporate blogger who's been writing her blog, *The Standards Game,* since September 2007.[57] We'll learn more about her blog in Chapter 10, but her nanoscopic topic? Industry standards in the field of electronic design automation. You get that? For more than a year, she's written a blog about the trials and tribulations of propeller-heads who are crafting mind-numbingly boring documents that explain how to get software from fierce competitors to cooperate. Care to hazard a guess as to her readership? Well, what if I told you that Karen has more than 1,800 RSS subscribers?

---

[56] Zen and the Art of Motorcycle Maintenance, Pirsig.

[57] http://synopsysoc.org/thestandardsgame/

Put another way, more than 1,800 people are so fascinated with what Karen Bartleson has to say about something as geeky as electronic design automation standards, that they've demanded to be notified the instant she publishes something new! That, my friends, is called *influence*.

As an executive who is contemplating a corporate blog, take a hint from Robert Pirsig. Have your bloggers write about a brick on a building on a street in their hometown. Learn from Karen Bartleson by choosing a topic that at first blush seems too narrow, but reveals a wellspring of stories once your blogger digs in. In both cases, those who are passionate about that narrow topic will find your blog; they'll tell like-minded friends, who in turn will subscribe to a valuable source of unique information.

And if you still don't believe in the power of nanoscoping, take a look at an online publication called *Bacon Today*—an entire Web site dedicated to "Daily Updates on the World of Sweet, Sweet Bacon."[58] In the first six months after its launch, *Bacon Today* garnered three hundred fifty-eight thousand unique visitors.[59]

New Media Tip: Focus on a niche
The narrower the topic, the deeper the audience.

New Media Content Producer

Most companies considering blogging turn first to their professional content creators. Although these folks are highly qualified to put a subject and a predicate together, their experience in creating good content for old media can weigh them down like a ball and chain. It's not that professional communicators can't be good bloggers. On the contrary, communication is the most important part of New Media; and having someone who is skilled at finding a topic, getting to the point, and making good arguments is a necessity. So, if your professional communicators can separate themselves

---

[58] http://bacontoday.com

[59] A "unique visitor" is a Web analytics term that refers to a someone who has come to your Web site over a specified period of time. The importance of the measurement is that a visitor is only counted once, independently of how many times they have returned to the Web page. For example if you visited Bacon Today's Web site once per day for the first six months, you would only be counted as one unique visitor during that time period.

from the ball and chain of old media content creation, by all means, implore them to blog. Otherwise, look elsewhere until they can escape the chain.

Look for your first bloggers from the ranks of those who speak with customers on a day-to-day basis—those who understand your products and services as well as, if not better than, your customers do. Initially, these candidates may come from sales, engineering, customer support, or even your customer-base, but no matter where you find them, potential bloggers must:

- read other blogs regularly;
- be natural communicators;
- have something unique to say;
- be ready to mix it up; and
- have the support of upper management.

Read Other Blogs Regularly

One of the most frequent mistakes companies make is diving straight into blogging without ever reading one. New Media channels may be cheap to implement, but they take time to master. You must do your homework and read multiple blogs from multiple sources regularly. Subscribe to RSS feeds using something such as Google Reader.[60] Interact with the bloggers that you read by leaving comments on their posts or exchanging e-mail with them. The easiest way to become a good blogger is to follow the work of other bloggers. You wouldn't take a test without studying, so why would you blog without reading other blogs?

Natural Communicators

Bloggers are natural storytellers. They are gifted writers who feel compelled to share their thoughts with the world. They are constantly learning, putting new ideas into perspective, and then sharing them with others. They frequently possess so much natural curiosity about their interests that they are driven to write about them. I've spoken with dozens of bloggers who've described how blogging changes their lives. Once they've chosen a nanoscoped topic, they

---

[60]   http://google.com/reader

see every life experience as potential fodder for their blog. Natural content creators are driven to produce—and they rarely see this activity as a burden.

New Media Tip: Not everyone is a blogger

If you approach employees to write a corporate blog and they see it as just one more burden to carry, they're *not* good candidates.

Forcing unwilling employees to be bloggers is tantamount to torture. Instead, find the frustrated writers in your organization, those who love to share their notes from conferences and are always sending out e-mails with links to great articles. The best candidates are those who are actually doing it already, they've just never had a name for it. However, this time, rather than their content getting buried in the *tyranny of the inbox*, it will be stored in a database for everyone to read at precisely the time that they need it. Once you find those people, you have the makings of your corporate bloggers.

Have Something Unique to Say

Not everyone is a good content producer. They may be able to write well, but if they don't have a unique point of view or a unique perspective, the blog posts that they write will be indistinguishable from others. Companies need bloggers with unique perspectives to share.

Take Bill Marriott, the chairman and CEO of Marriott International and author of the *Marriot on the Move* blog, for example. On February 5, 2007, he posted a story about the decision to eliminate trans-fats from all Marriott kitchens.[61] Rather than simply posting the fact, which any McPressRelease could have, he wrapped the news into a story of how things have changed over the years. He shared the fact that Marriott hotels served six-million pounds of French fries every year! Bill Marriott has been in the hotel business for many years; he has a unique perspective and, by sharing that perspective, he makes his blog different. There is only one person who is qualified to write Bill Marriott's blog: Bill Marriott.

New Media Tip: Content creators may be right under your nose

Who in your company offers such unique perspectives that even your own employees drop what they are doing to listen to them? Find them.

---

[61] http://www.blogs.marriott.com/search/default.asp?item=474238

Ready to Mix It Up

Disagreement is natural. If we always agreed with one another, our world would be a boring place to live. But for some reason, we shy away from disagreement or confrontation in our corporate communications. The corporate blog, however, is one of the best channels for you to make your company's case regarding the controversial subject *du jour*. Is there a raging controversy surrounding your industry? Tackle it. Is a competitor spreading FUD about your products and service? Mix it up. Corporate bloggers who are willing to hang their opinions out there are the most popular, because they are unique. In Chapter 10, I'll show you how controversial online conversations build audience sizes.

Have the Support of Upper Management

Convincing upper management to support blogs is only the first of many steps necessary to create a successful blogging program. Because blogging opens up online conversations, unintended consequences will inevitably arise and cause corporate heartburn. Perhaps a competitor calls your bloggers out to defend something that they wrote, or perhaps your bloggers addressed a product deficiency with more candor than your marketing department was comfortable with, but you must stay the course and support New Media efforts.

Take a deep breath. Relax. Then get the appropriate people into the room to discuss the issue. If your bloggers did something that violated the employee handbook or the New Media policy, reprimand them. If not, support them with every resource you possess. One of the worst things that can happen is for a blog post to show up on a corporate site and then mysteriously disappear. If your blogger is being transparent and thus building credibility, you cannot undermine that activity by removing a post from the site. The online community will revolt, causing more problems than those perceived originally.

Save yourself some time and a few blood pressure points. Address the incident appropriately online, learn from it, and move on.

Blog Well, Blog Often

From the perspective of inbound, search-based marketing, the corporate blog is the most important piece of content that a corporate Web site can have. Not only does it offer a place online for your company to tell its own stories, but also Google loves blogs. Type "Bill Marriott" into Google and take a look at his first result. Instead of finding his bland corporate bio, you'll find his blog.

New Media Tip: Your new mantra

- Google loves blogs.
- Google loves blogs.
- Google loves blogs.

Chapter Summary:

- New Media channels need new content.
- Good content tops the results of search engines.
- Blogs are inherently built for Search Engine Optimization.
- The narrower the topic, the deeper the audience.
- Online content creators are a special breed.
- Google loves blogs.

Chapter Eight

New Media Means New Management

Management is doing things right; leadership is doing the right things.

—Peter Drucker (1909–2005)

Beware the Land Grab

In the mid-1990s, as the World Wide Web expanded beyond university labs and into commerce, innovative people within companies raced to publish Web pages. Techies, who traditionally had nothing to do with corporate messaging, set up Web sites for internal *and* external audiences. It didn't take long for the marketers to cry foul—they were worried about unqualified writers interfering with the brand. The fear of inept employees communicating directly with customers proved too much for the *Traditionals* and they took over. Marketing staked its claim over the corporate Web site.

However, the battle for Web site control didn't stop there as another business unit, Information Technology (IT), pleaded its own case. Tasked with keeping communications systems running smoothly, IT maintained the Web servers, which were experiencing higher levels of stress as more content was published and more people started visiting. IT invested in new hardware and software to meet this growing demand, yet found the need insatiable as the Web became popular. The more money that the IT department spent trying to satisfy demand, the stronger their case became to control the corporate Web site.

Fast-forward to the present and the new economics of influence. Just as many early Web designers ignored corporate gatekeepers in favor of innovation, today's New Media early adopters are doing the same thing, with one major difference. Innovators today have extensive external options available. Let's say that IT can't respond quickly enough to install a Wiki or a user forum. Rather than throwing their hands up in frustration as they would have in the past, *Get-Its* can take matters into their own hands by building their own New Media platforms on third-party Web sites. This, in turn, causes more grief for the professional communicators who expect 100 percent control over company information and discover that it's being hosted outside the safety of the corporate firewall.

If controlling their own employees isn't enough to keep them up at night, user-generated content is seeping into corporate communications channels. Customers are discussing products and services in blogs, on podcasts, and through the creative use of online video. Customers are getting *official* support through *unofficial* channels such as third-party run user forums. Legal departments and *Traditionals* go apoplectic when faced with uncontrolled online conversations and will try every trick in their handbooks to stop them. But they're missing the point. Humans are, by their very nature, helpful. If someone needs help, there will always be others willing to provide that help. If an organization refuses to answer questions about products or services, someone else will be more than willing to do it for them. It's a simple choice. Do companies embrace these new technologies by acknowledging and using them, or do they attempt to quell them?

Executives around the world are wrestling with these questions, but few are answering them in a strategic way. Instead, they are letting the *Traditionals* fight over it. You must decide:

Is the future of your company's most important communications channel riding on the political savvy of your staunchest *Traditional*?

Let's take a look at some scenarios:

1. Jennifer, a talented young marketer, uses a screen capture package to record a product demonstration and embeds the resulting video into a corporate Web page. At three o'clock in the morning, IT Director Jerry is awoken from a sound sleep because the corporate Web server crashed. Jerry learns that some idiot from marketing published a

video onto a server not designed to support streaming video. Jerry orders the page taken down and then sends Jennifer's boss a nasty e-mail with a stern warning to never let it happen again. A few weeks later, IT issues guidelines for online video—and controls all future uses.

2. Tom has been in public relations for ten years. While reading his daily LexisNexis* report, he sees a blog post that mentions his company. After some digging, he's horrified to find that the blog is written by an employee who has been posting unnoticed for the past three months. A quick phone call to the blogger reveals that he has no experience talking to the media, has no clue about corporate messaging, and is actually sharing his opinion about products, services, and even competitors. Within minutes, Tom is on the phone to the blogger's boss, trying to figure out which of the two needs to be fired. Follow-up meetings are held to establish a plan. Since Tom is responsible for all public relations, he believes that he should control all blogging within the company.

   The first two situations are composite stories that I've lived through. This third one is verbatim with the names changed to protect the guilty.

3. Marketing launches user forums that encourage customers to post questions and employees to post answers. The tech support VP sees these forums and isn't pleased. She demands that one of her directors sends a group-wide message to express her displeasure. This is what it says (edited to protect the guilty):

Group Employees,

You may have seen the recent launch of so-called "User Forums" on the new microsite. Let me remind you that these sites are publicly viewable by industry press and analysts. At our company, only designated individuals are authorized as company spokespeople. As with other industry forums, our employees are not to post or respond on these forums unless explicitly authorized to do so by a member of the vice president's staff. If your customer is asking a question on a public forum, you are encouraged to contact them directly, but do not post a response in a public space. We all have a responsibility to protect customer and company intellectual property. If in doubt, talk to your manager.

As you can see, New Media causes smart people to say stupid things. As an employee seeking to help customers, how would you feel after receiving such a message? Or, as a customer, how would you feel posting questions on a neutered User Forum? No matter what happens, companies cannot allow corporate infighting to spill outside the firewall and tarnish company image and customer interaction. If one organization sets up a user forum and another declares war on it, the ultimate victim is the customer.

The barrier to entry for using New Media technologies is so low that departments experimenting with them are likely to step on other's toes in the process—unless they cooperate beforehand. Rather than allowing some twisted version of corporate Darwinism to determine your future, you must engage all business units when developing your New Media strategic plan. During these discussions, you must represent your most important constituents—your customers. Without an advocate in the room, they will suffer and thus so will your company.

"They're Contacting Our Bloggers"

I picked up the phone to hear one of my clients say, "Ron, our bloggers are getting e-mails from readers!"

Thinking that I was responding appropriately, I said, "That's great! We've established a new line of communications with customers."

Evidently, my response wasn't what she wanted to hear.

"We can't have private conversations happening between bloggers and the readers," she said.

"Umm, why not?"

"Because we need to know what they are saying. If they want to say something, say it in a comment. We need to put something on the blogs that prohibits readers from contacting the blogger directly."

I tried explaining that—for myriad reasons—readers might want particular conversations to remain private. But more importantly, I pointed out that customers are reaching out! Her bloggers are becoming influential—the best benchmark for corporate-blogging success!

She didn't buy it.

New Media is all about influence. *Traditionals* are all about control.

As an executive looking to foster the adoption of New Media, you'll take on dual roles. Some will see you as the *Champion of Influence*. Others will view you as the *Enemy of Control*.

Where to Find New Media Content Creators?

Where should New Media content creators come from? Product marketing? Marketing communications? Public relations? Product development? Which department has the skills to create good, repeatable content? Sales? Customer support? IT? The answer depends on three things:

1. Your organization and the types of products and services it produces
2. The corporate culture and its willingness to support change
3. The physical concentration of relevant content creation skills

Let's take a look at some business units to discuss the pros and cons of New Media ownership.

Public Relations:

The most common place to look for content creators is within your PR team. Whether internal or external, PR folks represent the epitome of content creation skills. They've spent their entire careers working with media. They have relationships, know how to influence the influencers, and have honed their skills in controlling their corporate messages. They know how to write in Standard English and have succeeded within the old economics of influence.

Yet their skills don't translate very well into a medium that demands transparency. PR people are often so focused on *controlling* the message that they're incapable of leaving anything to chance. Rather than being written for the journalist who in turn writes for the end-customer, New Media is written directly for the end-customer. PR people can do this, but they must unlearn what they know. Since writing for an online audience requires an intimate knowledge of the products and services rather than knowledge of how to position them, traditional PR people don't have all the skills to create New Media content. They can be invaluable members of the team, however.

Marketing Communications:

Marcomm is probably the wrong place to look for people to run New Media programs. Their old economics-of-influence skills are great for buying advertising, setting up trade show floors, establishing Web site tracking links, and publishing the corporate e-mail newsletter, but they just don't have the intimate product knowledge necessary to become credible members of the online community. Without the knowledge that is gathered through day-to-day contact with products or customers, Marcomm employees typically don't have the conversational experience required to build online credibility.

Product Marketing:

Product marketing is an area where New Media has a much higher probability of working—with specific caveats. Typically, product marketing managers know the ins and outs of their products. They've presented in front of customers and are used to conversing with them. The biggest challenge that they must overcome resides within their willingness to remove their rose-colored glasses. If product marketing managers are willing to admit that their products have warts, then they have a real chance at being successful with New Media. If not, they are not good candidates for the creation of New Media content.

PR, marketers, and product marketing round up the usual subjects when companies first look for New Media communicators. But if we step backward, two more departments must be examined: Sales and Customer Support.

Sales:

If the role of marketing is to deliver messages to the marketplace, then the role of sales is to engage in one-on-one conversations with customers. Marketing is designed to deliver messages from one-to-*many*. The sale of goods and services, especially expensive ones in the Business-to-Business (B2B) arena, requires the process of discussing one-to-*one*. In transaction-based businesses, where the goal is to drive traffic to a Web site and to then convert those visitors, marketing may be enough. However, if your company sells products and services that require more contact with buyers, distributors, value-added resellers (VARs), or end-users, marketing is only the beginning of a longer process. Once prospects have received marketing's messages, they'll need details. When they do, they seek to engage with people who are versed in the skills of one-to-one conversation instead of the art of one-to-many. By definition, the organization that excels in the art of one-to-one communication is your sales department.

Salespeople come in all shapes and sizes. The best are natural conversationalists. Take a look around your own sales organization for proof. The consistent top salespeople within your organization are engaging, understand your products, and can clearly state how your products help clients. They are extremely convincing and very good at what they do. Salespeople are trained in the art of persuasion. They are quick on their feet and can handle objections deftly. As the business unit with the most experience in one-to-one customer conversations, salespeople must be considered for the implementation of your New Media strategy.

Customer Support:

Customers have problems with your company's products or services. Who do they call? PR? Marketing? If they buy high-ticket items, customers might call their sales reps—especially in B2B transactions. If customers feel a need for escalation, they might even contact your CEO. However, in most cases, customers will call your customer support department.

Customer support is yet another business unit that has not only the skills to help with New Media content, but also solid technology behind it. Many companies manage customer support requests through ticketing systems and user forums, having already embraced online communications technologies for engaging with customers. Customer support reps are skilled in one-to-one communication with customers, and therefore your decisions regarding New Media can benefit from their experiences.

Who Should Control New Media Activities?

The problem with the proper adoption of these new channels is that New Media requires an interdisciplinary set of skills that has historically been distributed throughout the corporate hierarchy. Marketers typically don't have the detailed information, but know how to write well and make it look good. Product marketing and PR folks are predisposed to spin as opposed to being transparent. Although they can speak one-to-one with customers, sales and customer support folks aren't all that well versed in the creation of compelling content.

Perhaps one of these departments has the capacity to handle the job. Perhaps your company should reorganize and create an entirely new group. Either way, adopting New Media requires fundamental corporate changes that must be pushed from the top down to succeed. At a certain point, you must decide. Are your departments flexible enough to squeeze New Media functions into your old hierarchy, or should you reorganize to meet the needs of the new economics of influence? A third alternative may hold the answer. A new department, headed by a newly created C-level position might be the right fit for your organization.

The chief New Media officer would coordinate all corporate New Media activities. The job requires a rich set of interdisciplinary skills to determine when to *push* through old channels and when to *pull* through the new ones. The person must be a warrior, willing to fight through the rejections of the *Traditionals*. The person just might be you.

Hiring New Media Employees

As you look through your present organizational structure to find New Media content creators, you're likely to find fewer people than expected. Teams built to support the needs of the old economics of influence aren't the best place to search for New Media content creators. You need to find ways of injecting new skills into the hierarchy: either by training existing employees or by hiring those who are already predisposed toward New Media.

Hiring consultants to perform New Media training is one way to get your company up to speed on the nuances of these new channels. Buying hundreds of copies of this book and giving a copy to every employee is another way. However, those solutions will only take a company so far. Eventually, you must reconsider New Media job requirements for all employment candidates and adjust your hiring procedures accordingly.

Frequently, a company opens a job position, recruiters create a pipeline of candidates to fill that position and, after a lengthy series of interviews, a decision is made. More often than not, you'll have to choose between two candidates so strong that if your budget allowed, both would be hired. But in real life, you must make a tough decision.

What if there was a single question that nobody asked each candidate during his or her interviews? What if the answer to this simple question made it clear, beyond a shadow of a doubt, who the leading candidate was?

"What is your experience in the creation of online content?"

What if, unknown to your interviewing team, one of the candidates was a talented YouTube producer, or told stories through the use of animation, or had been producing a podcast about the impact of video games on pop culture for more than a year? Even if the content weren't relevant to the job position, wouldn't that be enough to sway your hiring decision? Without asking the question during an interview, however, your choice will be left to the proverbial coin toss, giving you a fifty-fifty chance of hiring this hidden talent or having it drop accidentally into the hands of your competitor.

Finding natural content creators is probably easier than you think. Remember the Net-Genners, the two billion people born between 1977 and 1997? Having grown up with the ability to manipulate digital data by ripping CDs or Photoshopping pictures, this group comes preloaded with innovative skills in creating compelling online content. You just need to ask them.

In his *TED Talk,*[62] outspoken attorney Larry Lessig[63] points out the differences between our generation and our kids'. "We watched TV," he said. "They make TV."

Net-Genners consider creating online content as normal. They may not consider their content creation skills to be anything extraordinary, therefore these skills never show up on their résumés. Therefore, interviewers must be trained to ask. The next time your company is hiring, ask about candidates' experiences with creating online content. Ask about their involvement with online communities. Find out if they have blogs, podcasts, or moderate user forums. You might just find a diamond in the rough.

1:9:90

Consumers of online content make up the largest segment of the online community. They're looking for information, opinions, or entertainment that can enhance their lives. The one thing that they aren't interested in doing, though, is creating new content.

There's a concept frequently discussed in New Media called "one:nine:ninety." Although more of a guideline than a rule, it speaks to the fact that if you take a random sampling of an online audience: one (1) person will be a genuine content creator—someone who maintains at least one online property such as a blog or creates online videos. Nine (9) people will interact with that content. They don't have any interest in creating original content, but love interacting with content creators by leaving comments on blogs, or answering questions in user forums. And ninety (90) people will happily consume the content created by the previous two categories.

---

[62] http://www.ted.com/index.php/talks/larry_lessig_says_the_law_is_strangling_creativity.html

[63] http://www.lessig.org/blog/

> But just because a random sampling of the online world produces this 1:9:90 split, it doesn't mean that your employee-base must be a representative sample. What if you can skew the results in favor of content creators through active hiring practices?
>
> Since creating good content is the key to New Media, it makes sense to hire natural content creators. What sort of competitive advantage might your company have if instead of 1:9:90, your mix was 2:18:80? How about 3:27:70?

Hire Storytellers

Most CEOs are very good at speaking with people and have interdisciplinary communications skills that cut across the one-to-one and one-to-many sorts. They understand their products and services and speak passionately about them. The best CEOs are storytellers.

The story is the most powerful communications device that humans have at their disposal. For some reason, human beings are hardwired to receive stories. We use them to connect with one another through common experiences. Who are the best teachers? Who are the people you like to talk with at parties? Who are the folks who could read the phonebook and you'd still listen for hours? They are the storytellers, those who weave facts into fabrics of interest. They illustrate with emotion, getting us to laugh, cry, or think—all things that we've been precluded from doing by professional content.

Hire storytellers to speak for your company.

Corporate Rock Stars: The Robert Scoble Effect

Under the old economics of influence, corporate communicators remained largely anonymous. Most marketing communications were written in first-person plural, portraying the corporation as a group-author as opposed to identifying a particular person. PR professionals were the ones to contact, based on their identification at the bottom of press releases. Even then, customers weren't encouraged to call, only journalists were.

New Media channels put faces on corporate content creators. No longer forced to deliver messages to the marketplace through third parties, you can use New Media channels to tell your company's own stories directly to customers, through real live people. The more popular these online personalities become, the more vulnerable they are to being wooed away.

Robert Scoble combined his love for storytelling and technology when he joined Microsoft in 2003. During the next few years, he became a prominent blogger and online video producer. Robert posted all sorts of content about himself and Microsoft employees. Sometimes, using a hand-held camera, he'd drop in on co-workers unannounced, and ask them what they were working on. Microsoft employees, passionate about their work, gladly reciprocated, gleefully discussing the projects that they were working on and how excited they were. More than anything else, these Channel 9[64] videos did something spectacular for Microsoft, they put a human face on the company, a corporation that was frequently portrayed as a cold, heartless behemoth based in Redmond, Washington.

Robert produced stories on everything. Sometimes he wrote glowing reviews about his employer. Other times he criticized the company, extolling the virtues of competitors such as Apple or Google. Much to Microsoft's credit, execs let Robert continue, despite those who wanted him reprimanded for breaking a cardinal rule of marketing and PR: *You should never say anything critical about the company that you work for.*

Human beings are funny creatures. Whenever we're asked to contemplate ramifications, we immediately zero in on the worst-case situation. But, Robert's criticisms spoke volumes to the various Microsoft contingencies. Rather than making the corporation appear weaker, they showed Microsoft as a vibrant company, filled with passionate people who cared about the products and services that they created. Robert's posts proved that people inside Microsoft were working hard to fix those problems because they cared. The more transparency Robert offered in his communications, the more human Microsoft's image became and the more popular he became.

The readership of Robert's blog, *Scobleizer,* exploded—further driving his fame.[65] Event coordinators begged him to speak at their conferences as more people heard about the innovative things that Microsoft encouraged him to do. In a very short amount of time, Robert became a rock star within the online tech community. As his visibility grew, so did his influence—the most important asset of the new economics of influence. And that's when Microsoft became the first company to experience another ramification of New Media.

---

[64] http://channel9.msdn.com/
[65] http://scobleizer.com/

The goal of any successful New Media content creator, such as a blogger, is to build trust with an audience. The more people who trust the blogger, the more influence that blogger wields. Corporations benefit from this influence through association. But what happens if your bloggers become so popular that they draw the attention of another company?

That's exactly what happened in February 2006, when Robert was wooed away from Microsoft by a startup firm called PodTech. The blogger who had built his reputation through creating content about Microsoft was leaving the company and, with his departure, Microsoft lost something else, too. The influence that he had achieved within the community for Microsoft was transferred to PodTech overnight.

High-tech companies have always had to deal with this danger. Any company that hires knowledge workers accepts the risk that much of its intellectual property leaves the building every night, carried in their craniums. To address this risk, high-tech companies stuff all types of creative legalese into employee contracts. Extensive paragraphs stipulate what is owned by the corporation and what is owned by the employee.

With intellectual property, we can see if an algorithm has been copied and pasted into source code. A jury can easily identify text that has been written in a blog. But how on earth do you limit an online reputation? How can you legally control the influence that your employees amass on your company's dime? The short answer is that you can't. Influence is a two-edged sword. The more influential your bloggers, the more the company gets to bask in their glow. Simultaneously, the more popular they become online, the higher the chance that someone with enough money will lure them away. It's one of the new wrinkles that you must consider as you adopt New Media technologies. As a footnote, Robert Scoble's situation has since played out a second time. In December 2007, eighteen months after transferring the light of his influence to PodTech, *Fast Company* magazine lured the beam toward them.

The more New Media content that companies produce, the more Robert Scobles will emerge online. The most successful will build audiences and gain influence that indirectly benefits their companies. These content creators will not need vast audiences to command large influence. Instead, through the power of small audiences, a few hundred loyal followers may be all that's necessary to create rock stars within your industry. In response, human resource departments around the world are going to have to rethink their employee retention strategies.

The Robert Scoble Effect only covers the influence that popular content creators have outside of the corporate firewall. However, those same bloggers influence those inside the firewall, too, which may not be appreciated. Take Marvin, the product marketing manager for a software product for example. He's worked hard on his product roadmap, carefully crafting the timing of new features that his product will gain over time. While he's attempting to execute that plan, Susan, a very popular corporate blogger writes a post describing common problems that her customers are experiencing with Marvin's product. She lists some features that her customers are asking for—features that don't line up with Marvin's carefully crafted product roadmap. Other bloggers outside the corporate firewall add their two cents to the discussion, suggesting their own prioritized list of features. The first company to incorporate these features will get their business. Now, the person who once had control over product development must deal with a new form of pressure. Real feedback from real customers in an open forum can throw a monkey wrench into the most carefully laid plans.

In this situation, Susan has incredible influence. She can argue that Marvin needs to throw away his plans and reprioritize. If Marvin refuses, he may have to convince his boss—who has been watching the entire conversation explode online. And while all of this is happening, with Susan's stock rising in the online community, human resources needs to account for this influence, making sure to provide Susan's manager with the most effective retention strategies available, such as additional salary, stock options, vacation, and other rewards—otherwise, she could throw her influence behind a competitor.

The introduction of New Media into your organization can create upheaval in ways that are hard to imagine. Influence, once tied to those who owned the printing presses, is now tied to corporate personalities who create content. That influence has value that others, including your competitors, will pay for. The Robert Scoble Effect introduces a new twist in the evolutionary relationship between employers and employees.

Note: On March 14, 2009, Robert Scoble announced that he was leaving *Fast Company* for a new employer. At Rackspace®, he'll be heading up a project called "Building 43."

Chapter Summary:

- New Media requires cross-organizational skills.
- Executives should prepare for political moves to control New Media within the corporation.
- The professionals may not be the best place to start looking for corporate content creators.
- Competitive advantage awaits those companies who can hire employees with online content creation skills.
- Companies can both benefit and suffer from the popularity of their employee content creators.

Chapter Nine

Calgon, Take Me Away!

o o o o o o o o o o o o o o o o o o o o o o o o o o o o o o o o o o o

Only you can prevent wildfires.

—Smokey Bear

Marketing guru John Wall uses the term "brain buster" to describe a concept that turns one's perceptions of the ordinary upside down.[66] Whether one comes in the form of a new product, service, or method, a brain buster takes time to get your head around. New Media technologies are frequently the source of brain busters because they're so different compared with their old media counterparts. They force people to rethink how to solve communications problems. I'm frequently the purveyor of brain busters as I explain New Media to executives, who are simply trying to understand how to adopt these quirky technologies into their corporate communications strategies.

This chapter is dedicated to a case study that demonstrates not only the use of the tools, but also how they solved a real business problem. It's a story of how an individual armed with New Media tools caused a PR nightmare for a Fortune 10 company, and how one company used New Media countermeasures to rectify the situation—all in less than twenty-four hours.

How's that for a brain buster?

---

[66] http://roninmarketeer.com, http://marketingovercoffeee.com, http://themshow.com

The Ranger Station Fire

Ranger Stations usually play the role of preventing fires as opposed to starting them. However, at 6:10 p.m. on December 9, 2008, a ten-year-old Ford® fan site called *TheRangerStation.com*^{SM} ignited a public relations fire that would rage online. Like all fires, it began with combustible material, namely a cease-and-desist letter that the site's owner received from the Ford Motor Company®. The letter demanded that Jim Oakes surrender his Web site and send Ford $5,000. Not knowing what to do, Jim sparked the blaze by posting his dilemma to *TheRangerStation*'s user forums.

Within two minutes of his post, "*TRS is being attacked by the Ford Motor Company*," the PR fire erupted into flames of angry comments that lapped at the big bad corporation and its asinine decision to pick on its own fans. The most cynical posts accused Ford of using the opportunity to recover revenue shortfalls in a down economy. Over the next twenty-two hours, Jim's post would receive 916 heated responses, which burned through his Web site's walls and ignited others.

Scott Monty awoke at 5:30 a.m. on Wednesday, December 10, 2008, no differently than he had for dozens of previous Wednesday mornings. As part of his morning regimen, the global digital and multimedia communications manager for Ford checked Twitter to see if anything needed his attention.[67] A late-night tweet indicated that something indeed had.[68] Twitter user Jregner said:

> *1:30 a.m. @ScottMonty This is about as bad as PR gets for Ford right now! Very bad move thats* [sic] *going to cause loss of sales: http://tinyurl.com/5o6jh8*

---

[67] Twitter is a free online service that allows its users to share messages in 140 characters or less. Called "microblogging," Twitter has become a platform for real-time online discussions that range from mundane to breaking news stories. It can be found at http://twitter.com

[68] A message on Twitter is called a "tweet."

The link lead to a Ford fan-site called *FocalJet*,[69] where another user had cut and pasted Jim Oakes's original post. In addition to JRegner's tweet, Scott got a Direct Message pointing to a similar post on yet another fan-site: *MustangEvolution.com*.[70] It didn't take long for Scott to discover that he'd awoken to a communications fire that had engulfed fan-site after fan-site overnight. He called Ford's associate general counsel before responding:

> *7:29 a.m. @JRegner Thanks for letting me know. I'm looking into that this morning.*

Ford committed to using New Media by recruiting Scott Monty to head the use of social communications channels. For the weeks before this, he'd been using the channels to explain Ford's stance on the so-called "Big Three Bailout Plan." Although Ford is considered one of the Big Three, Scott had been explaining the difference between Ford's finances and those of GM® and Chrysler®. Ford wasn't on the brink of bankruptcy and therefore it didn't need cash. Yet, at the same time, Ford did support the bill because of interdependence within industry supply chains. If GM and Chrysler failed, Ford's future could be jeopardized.

Efforts to spread this message paid off that morning with a front-page article in *USA Today*®—an accomplishment that Scott shared with his 5,600 Twitter followers:

> *8:32 a.m. Ford makes the front page of USA Today: Ford benefits from CEO's turn to road less traveled http://is.gd/aYTm*

But that's when Scott's day took a turn for the worse. As the online fan site communities awoke, they fanned the flames of *TheRangerStation* fire. More people commented about the situation on multiple user forums. Bloggers dog-piled onto the discussion, writing scathing attacks on Ford, along with others who microblogged snide comments on Twitter. As a direct result of Jim Oakes's original call-to-action, Ford's customer support department received more than a thousand e-mailed complaints.

Within hours, Scott was thrust into the role of firefighter staring at a raging PR fire—without enough facts to fight it properly. He attempted to knock it down through live Twitter updates:

---

[69] http://forums.focaljet.com
[70] "DM," in Twitter parlance, is a private message between Twitter users.

10:54 a.m. @pblackshaw I was made aware of it this morning and I'm tracking down our trademark counsel to weigh in on it. Not good.

10:55 a.m. @beadgergravling I'm on it. Getting our legal team's perspecive [sic] and trying to stop a PR nightmare.

11:13 a.m. @leeTrans @davidrinnan @Energy_Geek @ peterdavis @insideline_com I'm personally looking into it. Hope to have an answer soon.

11:23 a.m. @ContractorTalk I'm in discussions with our Chief Trademark Counsel about it right now. I'm none too pleased. #ford

That's when Scott did something that is unique to social media communications channels, a feat that would have been impossible even two years ago. Admitting that the fire was too big for him to fight alone, he called on his volunteer firefighters for help:

11:31 a.m. For anyone asking about the Ford fan sites and legal action: I'm in active discussions with our legal dept. about resolving it. Pls retweet

A retweet is probably the most powerful communications device in the social media world today. It's when one Twitter member retransmits another member's tweet. A retweet is an endorsement of sorts, where followers trust the original author enough to retransmit the message to the audiences who trust them. Nineteen of Scott's 5,600 Twitter followers responded by retweeting his message to their own communities, consisting of more than 13,400 people!

Meanwhile, Scott continued dousing flames.

12:17 p.m. @mdurwin @voltageblog I'm finding it's a much different story from our legal department …

12:29 p.m. @petertdavis It means we didn't get the full story from the site owners. There's a deeper issue in question. #ford

1:07 p.m. Re the Ford fan site: I'm finding that there was counterfeit material being sold on it. Trying to get clarity on the URL issue. #ford

With the fire still out of control, you might expect that Scott's attention would be totally consumed by it, but the record shows that he was still performing his normal daily duties—answering questions about the bailout, sharing fun Ford facts, and even tossing a little levity into the mix:

1:32 p.m. Excuse me for just one moment. CALGON, TAKE ME AWAAAAAYYYY!! Thanks. I'm all set now.

2:14 p.m. @davejohnston The irony with that ad is that Ford isn't taking any of the proposed loan money. http://is.gd/aSY1

4:03 p.m. @psadler And the Model T only got 12 horsepower with a maximum speed of 20 mph.

Between Twitter posts, Scott engaged in multiple conversations at the home office. The first involved his legal counsel, who explained that *TheRangerStation* was selling counterfeit Ford products—specifically decals with the Ford logo on them. He learned that the letter to Jim Oakes was an attempt to make him stop selling. The demands for the site and $5,000 fee were simply added as a legal scare tactic. Scott requested that the legal team separate the site issue from the counterfeit one. He knew that alienating Ford enthusiasts by taking down an established and popular site was not a smart decision. Legal staffers wrote another letter outlining strict rules that Jim Oakes would have to adhere to, including not selling counterfeit goods. Armed with a response in legalese, Scott worked with both the communications and legal teams to craft a more approachable public statement.

Crafting a corporate message is only half of the solution; the other half is deciding what to do with it. The easiest thing would have been for Ford to post a response and have Scott tweet links to that Web-based location. But Scott understood the dynamics of Social Media. *TheRangerStation* fire was fueled by a community's passion and therefore he needed an alternative to a cold corporate statement to reach them. Scott picked up the phone and called Jim Oakes directly. Scott described the events in an interview on the *For Immediate Release* podcast: *"I didn't want him to get blindsided by any of this and I just wanted to hear his side of the story and understand what his motivation was. And he was a really, really nice guy ..."*[71]

Evidently, Jim received the letter and panicked. He didn't have $5,000 and didn't want to lose his site. And so, he asked his supporters for help:

> *"And he was literally flabbergasted at the scope that this took on so quickly and did not intend to make any harm towards Ford or cause any trouble for us. He just wanted to do the right thing."*

The two chatted a little before arriving at an agreement:

> *"...I let him know what the lawyers were thinking and we came to an agreement and then, after our phone call he posted on his site what our conversation was about and then I submitted the official statement from Ford ..."*

At the same time as Ford was posting its official response, a new fire sparked as Twitter user BrettTrout said:

> *4:32 p.m. How do you repay your online evangelists? Well if you're Ford Motor Company, you step on their necks & demand $5,000 http://snurl.com/7r12q*

Scott immediately doused the flare-up with a message to his Twitter community:

> *4:34 p.m. @BrettTrout Please correct that. We've since remedied it http://tinyurl.com/6b7njd*

---

[71] www.forimmediaterelease.biz/rss.xml

4:44 p.m. @rgrosskett @NickLongo @digitalmlewis @ JeanneYocum @designmeme Ford's response can be found at the bottom of http://is.gd/b3h0

Immediately, the Twitterati began responding. Eleven minutes later, Scott was answering questions directly while also appealing to the power of the retweet:

4:55 p.m. @KrisColvin We're not shutting the site down; we're asking that they stop selling counterfeit material. #ford

4:56 p.m. Here is Ford's official response to the fansite cease & desist debacle http://is.gd/b3qd #ford Please retweet

This time, twenty-five of Scott's followers responded to his call, retweeting his message to twenty-one thousand more Twitter members!

Once the fire was contained, fireman Scott Monty spent the rest of the day soaking hot embers—answering questions and challenging inaccurate statements. Finally, he sent the 138th and final tweet of his day:

2:29 a.m. December 11th: @conniereece Zzzzzzzzzzzzzzz

The total time of the episode, from the origin of *TheRangerStation* fire to its containment, was twenty-two hours and twenty-six minutes.

No one perished in the blaze.

Lessons in Firefighting

TheRangerStation fire case study illustrates subtle points that executives frequently overlook when considering the adoption of New Media channels. From the power of user-generated content, to the speed at which the news spread, to the unique skills of Scott Monty, there are numerous lessons we can learn. Let's take a closer look at some of them.

Lesson #1: Everything Is Public

The first lesson has nothing to do with the story itself, but rather the data that was used to tell it. The point is that everything online is archived, and people with enough interest can mine that data for information. Executives looking to adopt New Media into their organizations can do the same thing by actively researching what's being said about their brands online. They can follow conversations on Twitter, read blog posts, and view user forum conversations. The data is available to anyone with access to a Web browser and can be surprisingly instrumental to your company. The question is whether or not you are willing to do the digital archeology work required to uncover it.

Lesson #2: Companies Don't Talk: *People* Do

People are essential to your New Media strategy. Unfortunately, most companies attempt to shoehorn technologies and responsibilities into a specific department such as marketing, PR, or the "Web Team" without an understanding of the interdisciplinary skills required by those employees to reach across the company. In this case, Scott Monty not only required the ability to communicate with clients, prospects, fans, and both his legal and communications teams, but he needed the ability to make quick decisions and implement them.

The following list describes traits that your New Media communicators require:

Listener

Without the ability to monitor social networks such as Twitter, Scott Monty never would have received the early warning necessary to control the fire.

Researcher

Rather than jumping into the fray, Scott had to get to the bottom of things first. Ford gave him access to the right people along with the authority to deal with them.

Multitasker

Instead of pursuing a single activity, Scott juggled the inner and outer worlds of Ford, getting to the bottom of the problem, crafting a solution, and working with the customer to implement it—all while keeping others informed of his progress.

Authorized Speaker

Without the authorization and trust of his upper management, Scott would have been hamstrung by the traditional bureaucratic red tape gumming up official corporate communications. Such a delay would have allowed the fire to spread further, intensifying an already difficult situation.

Human Communicator

Scott's ability to add a human touch to his comments put a face on Ford. Anyone who was following the story could see that he was working his tail off trying to get to the bottom of the problem. And finally, his personal call to Jim Oakes was probably the single most important decision that he made all day—an act preventing a potential "he said/she said" situation.

Humble Petitioner

Social Media is about people. People like to help other people, especially those whom they trust. Realizing that the problem was too large for any one person to tackle alone, Scott put his ego aside and asked for help. His calls for retweets multiplied his reach exponentially. Every person who retweeted one of Scott Monty's messages made it available to nearly seven hundred fifty additional people.

Warrior

Today, those with a keyboard and an Internet connection can cast their opinions far and wide. Just as Scott's role was to get Ford's message out, he also needed to defend it. By calling out bloggers and Twitterers who were spreading inaccurate information, Scott defended his brand appropriately.

Interdisciplinary Communicator

Like combustion fires, PR fires come in all forms. Each requires different sets of skills to extinguish it. Without his ability to understand legal, customer support, online communications, and long-term ramifications of decisions made under fire, Scott's efforts would have failed.

Lesson #3: Without Support, New Media Fails

Most corporate communications strategies are built around the concept of control. Long meetings are spent crafting perfectly tuned messages to be delivered from a corporate pedestal—and only certain spokespeople are authorized to distribute the approved messages. The system sufficed when only a few could afford to be publishers. But today, anyone can post to a fan site and thousands can send complaints, so new methods must be devised. Had Ford taken the traditional route—organizing a committee to determine how to respond—this situation likely would have spilled into the mainstream press, where the fire would have grown too big to handle.

Companies must support their New Media communicators. If "Calgon, take me awaaaaayyyy!" are the words chosen for that specific moment, then upper management must trust that they are the right words for the right time. If you refuse your bloggers that level of trust and authority, your company's New Media efforts are doomed.

The adoption of New Media channels into your organization promises to be a challenging—yet exciting—effort. Through proper use, they allow your company to connect with your customers in ways that were impossible just a few years ago. But with opportunity comes responsibility. The content injected into New Media channels can't be created by committee or by any other nameless and faceless entities. Real people communicating in real voices must feed those channels with content.

New Media is not about spending money. Instead, it's about how management allocates employee time and supports the use of that time. It requires executive oversight to reevaluate the roles of its present employees and then determine the best allocation of those resources to meet the needs of rapidly growing online communities.

What Is the ROI of Scott Monty?

New Media is dogged with the question of ROI. Let's turn that around and ask the same question about this case study:
- Scott Monty spent nineteen hours working on this problem.
- He investigated the situation.
- He ran several meetings.
- He made multiple phone calls (one to the site owner).
- He posted 138 times to Twitter.

- He asked for help and his followers spread his message to 32,332 others.
- He quelled the blaze in less than twenty-four hours.

You tell me. What was Ford's Return on Investment?

New Media Tip: Hire well

If you are ready to make the tough decisions about New Media, take a lesson from Ford and hire someone like Scott Monty. As Smokey Bear says, "Only you can prevent wildfires."

Chapter Summary:

- Online publications have the power to spread public relations nightmares overnight.
- Traditional PR response mechanisms may be too slow to respond to such situations.
- New Media technologies such as Twitter offer real-time response capabilities.
- Companies must prepare for such situations by authorizing employees to speak on the company's behalf.

Chapter Ten

Measure, Analyze, Rinse, Repeat

o o o o o o o o o o o o o o o o o o o o o o o o o o o o o o o o o o o o

Measure not the work until the day's out and the labor done.

*—**Elizabeth Barrett Browning** (1806–1861)*

It's All in the Analysis

Everything in business needs measurement, and New Media is no exception. By using free or paid analytics tools, you can piece together valuable insights about your company's online activities—both inside and outside the corporate firewall. Most organizations, though, spend more time and money on data collection and automatic reporting mechanisms than they do on data analysis. Collecting data without performing analysis is like buying a gold mine without extracting the gold. You may own property worth billions, but without mining, it's just another mountain.

Google's Analytics Evangelist, Avinash Kaushik, proposes that executives invest more in people than in the Web analytics tools required to gather that data.[72] Instead of spending lots of money on tools that crank out reports and filling people's e-mail inboxes with attachments that never get opened, he suggests executives allocate more resources to analyze the valuable data that free tools can provide. By hiring people to study this data, you'll be able to uncover stories to tell, find lessons to learn, and generate ideas that help advance your corporation's objectives.

---

[72] http://www.kaushik.net/avinash/

This chapter looks at real data. It shows how to put New Media data into perspective compared with other traditional Web analytics. By the end of this chapter, you'll have a solid understanding of the difference between old economics of influence and new economics of influence measurements. The former is based on the theory of large audiences and probability. The latter is built on the theory of small audiences and influence.

Pack the Room with Prequalified Leads

Godwin Maben is an electrical engineer who works for Synopsys, Inc. Synopsys sells software to electrical engineers who design Application Specific Integrated Circuits (ASIC) colloquially called computer chips. And if you think that computer chips represent a super-niche content area to focus on, consider the fact that Godwin is an expert in a subtopic of ASIC design—he's a guru in low-power ASIC design techniques. To put that in plain English, have you ever run out of battery power on your cell phone? Well, Godwin helps electrical engineers design chips that consume less power so that you can talk for longer times between battery charges.

On March 31, 2007, Synopsys launched the first corporate blog in the Electronic Design Industry (EDA) industry. The *Magic Blue Smoke* blog is highly technical because Godwin knows his audience, which consists of electrical engineers who are trying to squeeze as much power out of a chip as they can.[73] In his blog, he shares his thoughts on low-power design techniques, step-by-step engineering procedures, and computer programming scripts that he encourages his readers to use on their own chip designs.

By its first anniversary, *Magic Blue Smoke*'s estimated readership had grown to more than four hundred per week (two hundred RSS subscribers plus two hundred unique visitors). And before you call that a small number, consider that only a year after Godwin started his blog, more than two hundred electrical engineers worldwide were so fascinated with what he had to say about low-power chip design that they requested to be notified (subscribed via RSS) the instant he published something new. This is not only fascinating, but also significant, considering that *Magic Blue Smoke* is a corporate-sponsored blog, on a corporate site, written by a Synopsys employee. By being transparent about his

---

[73]   http://synopsysoc.org/magicbluesmoke

relationship with Synopsys and its products, Godwin lets his readers take this relationship into account. They still respect what he has to say, biased or not.

So what does this mean to Synopsys's business?

Let's take a closer look at Godwin's audience. Most of his readers have at least four-year degrees in electrical engineering. These electrical engineers not only work for companies that produce chips—Synopsys's target market—but companies with a need to build chips that conserve power. Because Godwin chose such a niche topic, he attracts very specific readers to his blog. The odds are that these readers represent prequalified prospects for the low-power products that Godwin supports.

Eight months after the launch of *Magic Blue Smoke*, a Synopsys account manager (AM) sought customer venues to present new features of Synopsys's low-power suite of tools. He cold-called an engineering manager at a Fortune 100 company that designs and sells millions of chips per year. During the conversation, the AM asked how many engineers the manager could round-up to hear the pitch. Knowing how busy his engineers were, the manager offered a guess of five-to-ten attendees—if he was lucky.

"What are you going to be presenting?" the manager asked.

The AM described an applications engineer by the name of Godwin who'd be talking about ...

The manager cut him off mid-sentence. "Godwin? As in Godwin the blogger?" he asked, before explaining how popular Godwin's blog was within his department. Instead of sending out an e-mail demanding people attend yet another vendor presentation, the manager crafted an e-mail encouraging his team to *Come Meet Godwin the Blogger*. The e-mail worked. Godwin presented to a standing-room-only venue, with an estimated audience of more than twenty people.

So, from an ROI measurement point-of-view, how much is a corporate blog worth? How much return does Synopsys realize through the fact that *Magic Blue Smoke* readers trust Godwin so much that they'll allocate time out of their busy schedules to go hear him speak—even knowing that his talk is part of a product pitch?

It's the power of influence—and influence affects the bottom line.

New Media Tip: Attract qualified customers

How much is it worth to your company to pack an enthusiastic group of prequalified customers into a room to hear a presentation about your product or service?

Get a 15 Percent Response Rate

On one hand, we can make good educated guesses about exactly who is reading our blogs. If we are very niche-focused, RSS gives us an indication of the types of people who are consuming the content. Although RSS is still an anonymous mechanism, allowing consumers to subscribe without us knowing too much about them except in the aggregate, that doesn't preclude our learning more about them.

Bloggers and their readers have a special relationship, and your company can benefit from it. Once bloggers build an audience, that audience offers valuable source information. Take Godwin's ultra-niche, self-selected group of low-power design engineers for example. On February 4, 2008, Godwin wrote a post entitled "Functional Simulation using UPF (Cont'd)." At the end of that post, he provided a link to a two-question online survey, using a free site (*surveymonkey.com*). At the time, *Magic Blue Smoke* had an estimated audience of two hundred sixty readers. Forty of them responded to his survey—translating into a response-rate of 15.38 percent—a number that would make any marketing executive drool. The point is that because these highly qualified prospects trust Godwin, they're willing to respond to his "call to action."

Godwin Maben is one of the pioneering corporate B2B bloggers who proves the power of presenting niche content in a transparent way. Through doing so, he has earned the trust of his readership, which can be measured:

- by the growth rate of his estimated audience;
- by the number of RSS subscribers;
- by the amount of people who will go out of their way to hear him talk;
- by the number of people who will respond to his call to action;
- And, of course, by the number of software licenses that Synopsys sells based on the trust that he's established with his audience.

New Media efforts are all measurable. Can your employees produce trustworthy content about your products and services as Godwin does? If so, you'll be able to put pencil to paper, and calculate exactly how much those efforts benefit your business.

Audience Analysis

Typically, a marketing manager will demonstrate the effectiveness of an online marketing campaign through Web hits, based on the old economics-of-influence theory that the more Web hits, the more effective the campaign. Marketing managers proudly display their Excel® spreadsheets containing tens of thousands of hits, yet when pressed for specifics, they really can't tell us anything about the people who were responsible for producing them in the first place or what those hits mean in terms of sales.

New Media requires a different way of looking at the numbers. Instead of choosing large metrics with minimal detail, New Media demands exploration of the smaller numbers, where distinct lessons can be gleaned. What can we ascertain about our visitors? Where are they coming from? How are they finding us? Which of our bloggers are our customers drawn to and which ones make them shy away? Most *Traditionals* rely upon the job security associated with presenting big, albeit useless, numbers. Executives looking to harness the power of New Media see power in the small numbers.

The Power of the Small Audience

When a vendor purchases a print or broadcast advertisement, the effectiveness of that ad is probabilistic in nature. For example, if the message is broadcast to one hundred thousand people, it'll only reach a tiny percentage of them. In *Back to the Future*, time-traveler Marty is stuck in 1955, but needs to get back to 1985. The only way to do so is to funnel the energy from a lightning strike directly into the flux capacitor. That's when Doc Brown says:

"Don't worry. As long as you hit *that* wire with the connecting hook at *precisely* 88 miles per hour, the *instant* the lightning strikes the tower, everything will be fine."

Advertisers face the same dilemma as Marty. A magazine ad can only reach people who are:

- holding that specific issue
- which is opened to that specific page
- and have looked directly at the ad.

Simple probability tells us that the majority of the target audience will *never* see the ad.

But now let's take a look at the online world. Your prospects are searching for a product or service that your company sells. They type a few descriptive words into their favorite search engine with the *intention* of learning about your products and services. When these Web site visitors arrive, what unique content do you have waiting for them? Do you have blogs written by experts, online videos of demonstrations, and user groups to answer common questions? Or do you have pretty brochures stuffed with perfect messages? What compelling content can you put onto your Web site to ensure your visitors never dream of going back to your competitor's brochure-based site?

The Web site visitors that find you through organic search are primed to learn how your products and services can help them solve their problems or meet their needs. If the information on your site doesn't satisfy that intent, then you've blown the opportunity.

Is it more effective to hit customers with your messages by happenstance through an advertisement or to provide them with the information that they need exactly when they need it? If you had to spend a dollar on marketing, would you rather invest it interrupting your customers' lives or providing a service to help them?

New Media Tip: Be helpful

The difference between old media and New Media is simple. The former is based on interrupting. The latter is based on helping.

RSS Revisited

In 2008, The Society for New Communications Research asked corporate respondents to evaluate the most important metrics for their social media initiatives.[74] In order of importance, the report revealed the following list:

---

[74] http://sncr.org/

1. Search engine ranking
2. Number of hits/unique visitors
3. Targeted audience awareness of the program
4. Blog search engine rankings
5. Incoming links
6. Bottom line increase
7. Positive/negative nature of blog posts or comments
8. **Number of RSS feed subscribers**
9. Number of comments on blog/podcast
10. Ratio between postings and comments

These rankings illustrate how those who rate the success or failure of their New Media campaigns still don't have a fundamental understanding of what these measurements mean. Until they do, corporate adoption of New Media channels will remain a challenge.

The first problem arises when RSS is listed as the eighth-most important metric on the list—proving that it's probably the most misunderstood measurement tool in all of New Media. I've had the opportunity to speak with hundreds of executives over the past two years, and less than 5 percent of those I've polled from the front of the room can even identify the RSS Feed's orange and white symbol—let alone actually use it. Given this fact, it's no surprise that traditional marketers rank RSS so low when trying to determine the success or failure of their New Media efforts.

RSS is about trust. Someone who opens up an RSS channel to your content is saying, in a very simple way, "I trust you." An RSS subscriber represents a person who's telling your company that she values the information so much that she's willing to open up a special content channel for you—something that's not to be taken lightly. She trusts that the blog will provide her with the same quality of content that she's been sampling. She trusts that she'll receive content at the same frequency by which she originally sampled it. And lastly, she expects your company to respect that trust and to not throw garbage into this trusted channel. If the company abuses this trust, she'll do something that is impossible to do if she subscribed to the company's e-mail newsletter—she can unsubscribe instantly and without your permission.

New Media Tip: Respect the trust subscribers have given you

RSS puts the relationship power into the hands of the subscriber. If the subscriber decides to unsubscribe from your feed, your company will never know about it and, more importantly, you'll never know why. Treat your subscribers with the respect that they have given you.

RSS subscribers are by far the most important people in the B2B marketing mix. They have self-selected themselves as associated with your product, service, or brand. They have opened up a trusted channel for you and—as long as you respect that trust—they'll keep you around. What could be more important than customers who love to hear from you so much that they use technology to listen actively for anything new that you have to say?

The Seesaw Effect

The introduction of RSS feeds into corporate communications strategies introduces a new wrinkle. If I opt to subscribe to an RSS feed of your content, then I never need to return to your Web site again to retrieve that content. By accepting your offer to receive content through RSS, I have instantly closed *my* eyes to *your* site. At first glance, this looks like bad news, since my once-frequent visits will drop off your Web analytics reports. Traditionals hate to hear this for two reasons:

1. They love to show graphs of Web traffic going up and to the right.
2. If people stop visiting the site, then there is no way to track their actions through carefully crafted tracking links.

And they're missing the point. Rather than evaluating this effect negatively, it should be seen as a way to learn more about your customers. By adding RSS to your Web site, you have given visitors a way to self-categorize themselves into two groups:

1. Those that want to consume content on your Web site without any commitment
2. Those who are committed to reading your corporate content through their RSS reader rather than your Web site

The upside of this categorization is that for every lost visitor, a newly qualified content consumer is created. The seesaw effect is that as the number of RSS subscribers goes up, the visitors to your Web site go down. Therefore, even though the number of Web site visitors drops by each RSS subscriber added, the average size of the audience for your content doesn't. The net result is that your audience doesn't go away—it just shifts. Let's take a look at some real data to illustrate this point.

Whenever a company starts a New Media project, it must include measurements as part of the plan. I recommend that companies venturing into New Media projects make a commitment to measure frequently enough to paint a picture, but not so frequently that data collection becomes a burden. As a rule of thumb, weekly measurements are fine for New Media projects.

For blogs, I recommend that companies measure the following metrics:

- **Unique Visitors**—This measurement only counts a visitor once. If a visitor comes back to the page a second time during the week, he or she is not counted twice.
- **RSS Subscribers**—The number of people who have actively chosen to subscribe to your content through an RSS reader such as Google Reader
- **Number of Comments**—Two measurements: the number of comments per blog post and the total number of comments for the entire blog
- **Number of Blog Posts**—the total number of blog posts
- **Age of the Blog in Weeks**—the length of time that the blog has been written. This number can be used to calculate things such as the frequency of posts (posts/week).

Once this data is collected, it's important to plot it over time. Without doing so, trends and patterns will be very hard to see.

We are fortunate to have real data from Karen Bartleson's blog, *The Standards Game,*[75] to illustrate these points. Figure 10-1 graphs RSS subscribers over the blog's first seven months:

---

[75] http://www.synopsysoc.org/thestandardsgame/

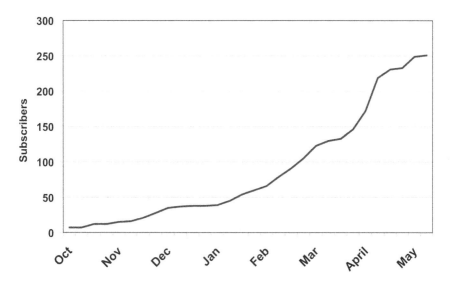

RSS Subscribers

Figure 10-1: RSS Subscribers to *The Standards Game* blog

Take a close look at the data. As you can see, the number of RSS subscribers rose at a moderate yet consistent slope for the first five months until the growth rate accelerated in February/March, before tapering off between March/April. Then, toward the end of April, the number of subscribers shot up again, and then returned to its natural growth rate.

Data by itself doesn't tell us anything special, but data in context does. A story is hidden behind these up-ticks in subscribers, but it can't be seen without looking at more data—such as the number of unique visitors to Karen's blog.

Unique Visitors

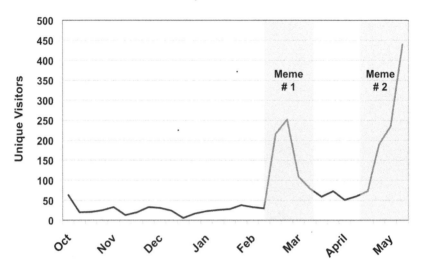

Figure 10-2: Unique Visitors to *The Standards Game* Blog
with Memes Highlighted

Isolating the number of unique visitors to Karen's blog, Figure 10-2 shows how the rise in RSS subscription rates coincides with two rapid increases in unique blog visitors. On two different occasions, March and May, more unique visitors read *The Standards Game* than at any other time in the blog's short history. So, what happened to drive this traffic? What is the story behind these numbers?

It's called a *meme*. A meme is a special online conversation that's charged with lots of energy. It could be the hot topic of the day, the event of the week, or the story of the year, but—whatever it is—people are talking about it online. If these online conversationalists have blogs, they're posting about it. If they don't have their own blogs, they're leaving comments on other's blogs. During the latter part of February 2008, *The Standards Game* became ground zero of an EDA meme.

On February 20, 2008, Karen wrote a post entitled "On the road to a single standard verification library." The post kick-started a conversation that reverberated throughout the tiny chip design community. Although the actual conversation is beyond the scope of this book, the resulting meme caught the attention of blogger J. L. Gray, who posted a critical assessment of Karen's post on his *CoolVerification* blog.[76] For almost three weeks, this meme continued, with blog posts and comments flying around until the topic eventually ran out of steam. At the peak of the frenzy, the number of unique visitors to *The Standards Game* rose from 30 to 252, growth of 620 percent! After three weeks, the number of unique visitors dropped back to a new base level, remaining significantly higher than the previous one. For the six weeks following the first meme, the average unique visitor count to *The Standards Game* was sixty-six, more than doubling the previous average. Memes are a very important part of growing your blogger's audiences and subsequently the influence that they have in your industry.

Lightning struck again on April 24, 2008, when Karen wrote another post entitled "Verification Standards Working Group is Launching!" which set-off a second meme—one that propelled the number of unique blog visitors to new heights.

Now go back and take a look at Figure 10-1 to see the rest of the story. During the first meme, the blog experienced an inrush of unique visitors as bloggers such as J. L. Gray linked to it and engineers forwarded. That's when something subtle but important happened. Some of these new readers found the content so compelling that they decided to subscribe to it via RSS. The seesaw effect kicked in, dropping the number of unique visitors by at least the number of new RSS subscribers and the audience size stabilized.

There is one last measurement that companies should track with regards to their bloggers: the "Estimated Audience," which is determined through the following equation:

Estimated Audience = Unique Visitors + RSS Subscribers

By adding these two numbers together and plotting the results, companies have a great tool by which to measure a blog's success.

---

[76] http://www.coolverification.com

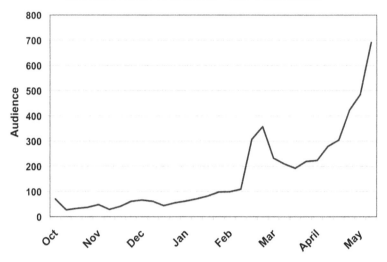

Estimated Audience (Uniques + RSS Subscribers)

Figure 10-3: Estimated Audience of *The Standards Game* Blog

Figure 10-3 clearly illustrates a blog with a growing audience. For the first five months, *The Standards Game* struggled to get to a point where one hundred people viewed it on a weekly basis. But during months six through eight, its audience grew seven-fold, fueled by two powerful memes as more and more people found *The Standards Game* to be a worthwhile place to learn about emerging EDA Verification tool standards. As a result, Karen Bartleson and Synopsys had established themselves as very influential members of the online EDA community. They had grown an audience that earned influence. Much to the chagrin of the *Traditionals*, that influence is measurable.

Meme Management

Memes are a very powerful force online, yet most companies are not ready to react to or benefit from them. Independent of whether your company is referenced positively or negatively within the context of a meme, it's important to own a place online for your company to participate in it. Without such a place, your company won't be able to:

1) React and offer your side of the story
2) Benefit from the swell of unique visitors who'll be drawn to your site to see what you have to say

3) Capture the hearts and minds of those who might be converted to RSS subscribers—your most qualified prospects and staunchest supporters

A corporate blog is a great place to participate in an industry meme.

Memes Boost Everyone's Audiences

J. L. Gray was one of the first EDA industry bloggers. As an electrical engineer with a specialty in ASIC verification (just as Godwin is a specialist in low-power design), he started writing his *CoolVerification* blog on July 25, 2005. J. L. is also the established EDA blogger who took issue with Karen's February 20 post, kicking off meme #1 that fueled the growth of her audience. But Karen wasn't the only beneficiary of the audience boost. J. L. too saw a change in his audience, which in turn boosted his influence within the engineering community.

Figure 10-4 compares the RSS subscriptions of *CoolVerification* and *The Standards Game*. From October 2007 through January 2008, J. L.'s subscriptions appear flat. As January of the New Year arrives, RSS subscriptions see a modest growth rate, as an average of 2.66 subscribers are self-selecting themselves per week. During the three-week period beginning February 20, though, this rate grows to 6.33 new subscribers per week, a 137 percent increase simply because he took issue with some of the things that Karen said in her blog. 6.33 RSS subscribers per week may not sound like a lot, especially when compared with millions of Web hits, but think about it in the context of this situation. Three short weeks after posting his commentary, J. L. had added nineteen new RSS readers to his subscription ranks. In other words, nineteen new electrical engineers gave him their trust and thereby increased his influence over the engineering community.

Unique Visitors

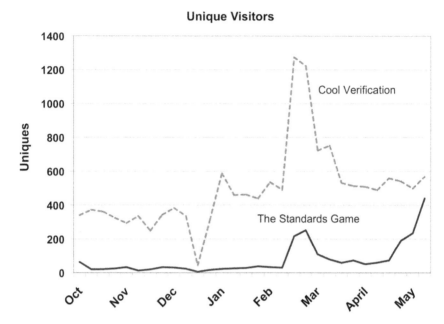

Figure 10-4: Overlay of Unique Visitors From Both
The Standards Game and *Cool Verification* **Blogs**

Because RSS subscriptions require action on the subscriber's behalf, they usually take longer to develop. Unique Web site visitors are a different story. Simply clicking on a link that a friend sends via e-mail or a blogger adds to a post is all that's required to become a visitor, and so those numbers are more volatile. Figure 10-5 shows the dramatic swing in the number of unique visitors that read J. L. Gray's blog. Within one week of the beginning of the meme, the number of unique visitors went up 159 percent, from 491 to 1274. To put this into perspective, within one week, 783 new people came to check out what J. L. had to say about the topic, more than doubling the readership of any of his previous blog posts.

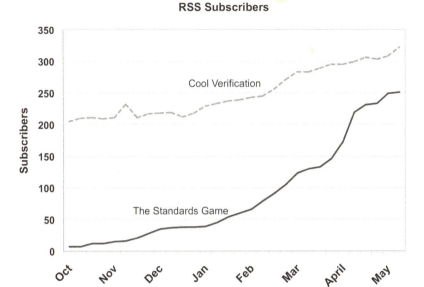

Figure 10-5: Overlay of RSS Subscribers From Both
The Standards Game and *Cool Verification* **Blogs**

Lastly, by adding up the RSS subscribers and the unique visitors, Figure 10-6 gives us an estimation of audience size. For the six weeks prior to meme #1, J. L.'s estimated audience averaged 733. For the six weeks after the meme, his average readership was up 12 percent to 822. This single meme had added an average of eighty-nine new readers to the *CoolVerification* blog—thus adding eighty-nine more people to those who J. L. influences.

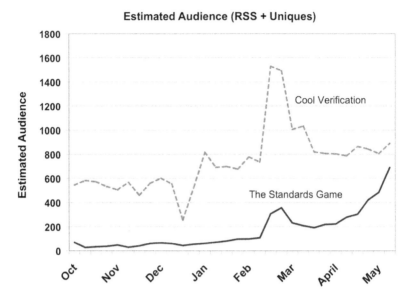

Figure 10-6: Overlay of the Estimated Audiences for Both
The Standards Game and *Cool Verification* Blogs

What Is the Return on Influence?

Karen Bartleson increased her average audience by 138 readers after the first meme. J. L. Gray increased his by 89. As a result, both increased their relative influence on the communities of electrical engineers that they each serve. If we take a look at this from a business point of view, what was the return on investment? Was it worth the investment of a few hours time for each of these engineers to share their thoughts with the world? Neither spent any money, but both invested their time. For the amount of time invested in writing and responding to each other's blogs, each gained measurable influence. What was the Return on Investment for these activities? Or perhaps we should ask a different question. "What was the Return on *Influence?*"

Acceleration

Once your corporate blogger has some experience and has started growing an audience, it'll be time to start looking at other metrics such as "acceleration," which is defined as the total number of blog comments divided by the total number of blog posts.

By comparing the ratio of comments to posts, acceleration offers an objective way for determining how engaged your audience is with your content. The rule of thumb is that a comment-to-post ratio should be at least 1.0; meaning that on average, for every blog post, there is at least one comment. Of course, the higher the number, the more engaged the audience, but a 1:1 ratio is something that companies need to be mindful of when determining the success of their corporate blogs. An acceleration calculation greater than 1.0 is good while a figure less than 1.0 is not. Acceleration is a nonemotional way to weed your corporate blog garden.

Take *Magic Blue Smoke* for example. By May of 2008, Godwin had written thirty-eight posts in eighty-three weeks and had generated sixty-eight comments. Sixty-eight comments divided by thirty-eight posts yields a comment-to-post ratio of 1.79, which is well above the 1.0 rule of thumb. Compare and contrast these results with that of fellow Synopsys blog *Inside Protocol Verification* (IPV), a team blog written by five bloggers. Between IPV's launch of November 27, 2007, and May of 2008, the team had written thirteen posts in forty-nine weeks, generating two comments for an acceleration figure of 0.27. Clearly, *Magic Blue Smoke*'s audience was much more engaged (actually 6.62 times more engaged) than the IPV audience.[77]

Using Acceleration to Increase Audience Size

The results of The Society for New Communications Research report shows that acceleration (listed as "comments/post ratios") holds the last spot on the prioritized list. Similar to RSS, its ranking demonstrates a lack of understanding. Comments are an important way to determine how engaged an audience is with respect to your content because audiences speak through comments. Through them, your prospects and customers speak directly to your blogger, expressing what they like and what they don't. Therefore, it's important that bloggers monitor comments closely—not from a defensive perspective, but from a learning one. Periodically, corporate bloggers should sift through their archives and review the number of comments for each post. The topics with the most comments represent the topics that most interest your customers. By spending more time talking about subjects with high numbers of comments and shying away from those with the least, corporate

---

[77] Synopsys learned from the data and discontinued the Inside Protocol Verification blog

bloggers can narrow in on the subjects that readers are begging to read about. The more that's written on those subjects, the more others will read and comment. As a result, audience growth becomes a self-fulfilling prophesy. The more comments, the larger the audience, the larger the audience the more influence the blogger develops.

New Media Tip: Let your customers tell you what they want

Think of comments as having a direct view into the thoughts of your most influential customers.

Acceleration as Competitive Data

Comments and posts are public information, which brings up an interesting opportunity for competitive analysis. Do your competitors have blogs? What is the acceleration of each of them? Are their acceleration numbers higher or lower than 1.0? What topics draw the most comments? Are their customers more interested in some topics than others? By studying the acceleration of your competitor's blogs, you can generate a picture of their audience's involvement. Take a look at the posts with the most and least comments and you can see the subjects that they are interested in and the ones that they aren't. All of this information is publicly available and can be used to launch your own blogs, cover the best topics, and ultimately grow your company's influence.

However, that's only if you've hired someone whose job it is to monitor and report the data.

Publicly Available Data and Analysis

So far we've used Web analytics and observation skills to determine the effectiveness of your corporate blogs. Most of the information that we've used is private data that is hidden behind the firewall, but there are a slew of free sources that can help you measure public data about your company. Would you like to measure your corporate brand online? How about your competitor's? What are the memes in your industry? How are they affecting the overall perception of your brand? Answers to questions such as these can be acquired with a moderate amount of digging. Here's an example.

In Chapter 4, I introduced the "Diet Coke and Mentos" video created by two soda pop pyrotechnicians from *Eapybird.com*. The video moved the brand needle of two multinational brands even though there was no official relationship established between all of the players. Most online video sites publish the number of views that a video has gotten, so there's no question that ten million views of the video had an effect on these brands, but can we measure how much the needle actually moved?

Viral videos are similar to the month of March; they come in like a lion and go out like a lamb. In the beginning, the number of views surge, as friends send links to other friends, who in turn send links to even more friends until at some point something happens to slow the growth. Perhaps the novelty wears off, a secret is revealed, or people have just moved on to the next viral video. Nevertheless, whatever causes interest to wane, one thing is certain; viral videos are like memes that come into existence in a big way and then trickle out. The question is whether or not they leave any measurable changes in their wake?

Google Trends is a free service that offers businesses a way to measure buzz from two different angles:[78]

1. It tracks the keywords that people are searching Google for
2. It tracks the same keywords that are found in Google News.

Therefore, by typing your company's name into Google Trends, a figure-of-merit, let's call it a Search Engine Index (SEI), is calculated that represents how many times people are searching for that term and how many stories are being written about it. This figure-of-merit can be plotted over time, going back as far as five years to make comparative measurements.

Let's perform a Google Trend analysis on "Diet Coke" vs. "Mentos."

---

[78] http://trends.google.com

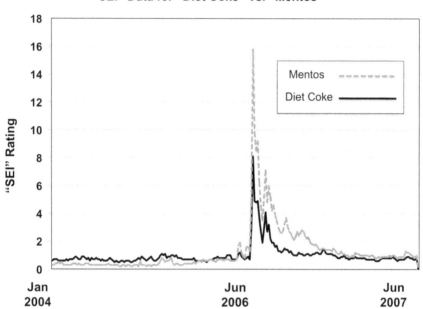

"SEI" Data for "Diet Coke" vs. "Mentos"

Figure 10-7: Overlay of Search Engine Index (SEI) Measurements for "Diet Coke" vs. "Mentos"

Figure 10-7 illustrates that for the 125 weeks leading up to June 2006, the average Search Engine Index (SEI) score for "Diet Coke" was 0.74 compared with 0.48 for "Mentos." One week after the video's release, however, keyboards across the globe drove these SEI figures up 994 percent for "Diet Coke" and a whopping 3,190 percent for "Mentos." Remember, this spike had nothing to do with what these international brands did on their own—rather it was because two New Englanders recorded themselves dropping candy mints into bottles of soda and putting the spectacle to music! We can call this an example of a Super Meme!

Since the spike in June, both SEIs have finally settled back to an equilibrium point. Over the last 53 weeks of our sample, "Diet Coke" has averaged 0.80 (up slightly from its 7.7 percent pre-video result), but surprisingly, "Mentos" is being typed into a Google search 129 percent more (1.02) than its pre-video score. Put another way, for the 125 weeks prior to the video's release, the term "Diet Coke" was typed into the Google Search Engine 35 percent more times than "Mentos." Today, "Diet Coke" lags "Mentos" search volume by 27 percent.

There's another public way to view the data: through typing "Diet Coke" and "Mentos" into the two most popular search engines: Google and Yahoo. Two years after the release, the fun nucleation reaction still holds substantial top ten spots in both Google and Yahoo searches.

	"Diet Coke"	"Mentos"
Google Top Ten Results	3,8	3,4,7,8,9,10
Yahoo Top Ten Results	10	3,4,5,6,7,9

Lastly, it's important to note that Eepybird.com isn't the only site driving these results. A YouTube search for the term "Diet Coke and Mentos" yields 6,870 videos. This story lives on as other soda pop pyrotechnicians worldwide record themselves performing similar feats.

Perfetti Van Melle and Coca-Cola brands have benefited greatly from these videos. A research study by the Society for New Communications Research reported that:

> *"Mentos tallied a staggering 215 million mentions of its product in TV, print, or radio stories over the past nine months, and estimates the free publicity was worth $10 million to the company—half its annual marketing budget. Sales climbed 20 percent … Sales of Diet Coke, which had been flat for some time, spiked between five and 10 percent, the company's interactive director told MediPost."*[79]

The data is there for the gathering. You can measure anything with New Media.

---

[79] New Media, New Influencers and Implications for Public Relations: A Research Study by the Society for New Communications Research With the support of the Institute for Public Relations & Wieck Media. Page 20. http://sncr.org/2008/08/06/changing-patterns-of-influence-through-social-media-explored-in-new-research-report/

New Media Tip: The information is out there waiting for you to find it

Chapter Summary:

- Most companies put more emphasis on data collection than analysis.
- New Media is not only measurable; it is by far more measurable than the media that came before it.
- New Media seeks a small, targeted audience as opposed to large general one.
- Most marketers still don't understand New Media measurements.
- RSS causes your Web hits to go down, but your qualified audience to go up.
- Memes grow audiences.
- Some Web metrics, such as acceleration (comment-to-post ratios) are public, thus can be used for competitive analysis.

Chapter Eleven

Knit One, Purl Two

o o o o o o o o o o o o o o o o o o o o o o o o o o o o o o o o o

To infinity and beyond.

—*Buzz Lightyear*

In 1991, a young computer scientist by the name of Tim Berners-Lee wrote an e-mail that described something that he called the World Wide Web. His idea was revolutionary. Before his so-called "Web," we shared documents by making electronic copies and transferring them from computer to computer. Berners-Lee, however, suggested an alternative method—to link documents together through something called a "hyperlink." It wasn't long before an interwoven collection of hyperlinked documents made his World Wide Web a reality.

We've come along way since Mr. Berners-Lee wrote that e-mail. We blog, we podcast, and we publish online video. We post comments, we Twitter, and we share our lives via social networks. We praise our favorite products and criticize those who disappoint us. And in the process, we've established an array of online relationships, where we share our opinions, and learn from one another.

It's easy to see the opportunities afforded individuals through the use of New Media channels. Up until this chapter, the goal of this book has been to extend that notion to business communications—regardless of whether your business falls into the B2C or B2B category. This chapter marks a transition point, as we shift our focus from foundation-building to New Media channel construction. It discusses two phases that must be accomplished if your company is to be successful in its New Media efforts: the New Media Audit and the New Media Plan.

New Media Audit

New Media channels come in three flavors: Listening, Talking, and Participating. The easiest and least risky way for companies to start learning about New Media is to monitor the online conversations that are occurring about your organization. By carefully orchestrating some of these free listening technologies, your company can assemble a comprehensive picture of your company's online reputation.

One way to create this picture is to perform a New Media Audit, an effort that has two goals:

1. To immerse your company into the online world and learn about it
2. To determine how your company wants to participate in the conversation through the riskier talking and participating channels

When your company decides to move to the next step, the New Media Audit will become the basis for a New Media Plan. There are no shortcuts. Audits come before execution. Without understanding what's out there, jumping pell-mell into New Media conversations is like running full speed into a darkened forest without a flashlight or a helmet.

Tribes taught us how we as humans like to associate ourselves with like-minded people. Edelman showed us that we trust "people like us." We like to associate ourselves with brands—perhaps your brand—where we discuss the things we love about your products and services and we commiserate on the things we hate about them. But no matter what our motivation is, we are likely talking about your brand, online, to others who care. The goal of the New Media Audit is to find where we hang out online. Before your company can engage with our communities, you need to know more about us, such as:

- How do we communicate with one another?
- What are we saying about your company?
- What are we saying about your competitors?
- What industry-related memes are occurring?
- What are our favorite New Media channels?
- What blogs do we read?
- What podcasts do we listen to?
- Which Social Media sites do we frequent?
- What are the customs for our online communities and what jargon do we use?

- How can your company engage with us without annoying us?
- The answers to these questions are readily available through the use of free online tools. Extracting them requires a corporate investment of time. If your company decides to invest that time, here are some simple steps that you, (or one of your diligent employees) can do to determine your company's online reputation:

1. Get a detailed Web analytics report for your corporate Web site from the head of your IT department. Look for things such as unique visitors over time, referring pages, and inbound links from other Web sites. Study this data. Look for patterns. By understanding this data, your company will have a head start on finding the communities that are talking about you online and what keywords they are using to find you.

2. Put together a list of at least ten keywords/key phrases that your constituencies are using to find your online communities. "Hell's Angels," for example, might be a good choice if your company is in the motorcycle business. Look back at your Web analytics report and compare these keywords with the most common ones that your customers already use to find your Web site. Are they the same? Is there anything surprising to note?

3. After you've listed these keywords, use your RSS feeds to monitor what people are saying about your company—in real time. Enter the keywords into:
   a. *Google News Search* and subscribe to the resulting RSS feeds using Google Reader.
   b. *Google Blog Search* and subscribe to the resulting RSS feeds using Google Reader.
   c. *technorati.com* and subscribe to the resulting RSS feeds using Google Reader.
   d. *search.twitter.com* and subscribe to the resulting RSS feeds using Google Reader.
   e. *flickr.com* and note how many people have published photos tagged with those keywords? Are any special groups set up for these keywords?
   f. *youtube.com*. How many people have published videos tagged with these keywords? View some of them. And pay attention.

    g. *del.icio.us.com*. How many people have bookmarked information about your company or its products? Subscribe to the resulting RSS Feeds with Google Reader

    h. *iTunes*. How many podcasts and video programs do you find on your subjects? Listen to them. Take notes.

The data gathered through this process will only reveal the tip of the iceberg. Now comes the hard work—getting a feeling for the mass below the surface and gaining an understanding of what it means. Follow the leads and take notes. Be thorough in your investigation. At first, the task may seem overwhelming as you uncover lead after lead, but have faith. You'll be rewarded for all of this work later. Bit by bit, blog by blog, community by community, a picture will emerge that depicts how the Social Web views your company. Before starting this effort, your company will have no idea whether the picture will look like a Degas, a Rembrandt, or a Picasso, but no matter what, it will offer a raw look at your company's online reputation. Often the results of this exercise are shocking, because for the first time, corporate executives are presented with raw, unfiltered commentary about the good, the bad, and the ugly of their companies—stuff that has likely avoided detection by your company's clipping services.

It might take a couple of weeks to sift through all of the content, but soon after starting, recognizable patterns will emerge. The same names of outspoken members will appear in multiple online communities. Do you recognize any of these names from the offline world? Did you know how active they were online? Once the New Media Audit is completed, your company will have the information by which to move onto phase two: building a corporate New Media Plan.

The New Media Plan

The New Media Audit identifies the communities that talk about your company, gathering details about those communities and the members who frequent them. It describes their customs and gives your company the information by which New Media decisions can be made, for example, by identifying some communities that may not be appropriate for your efforts. By carefully selecting places for your company to focus online, a New Media Plan will emerge.

A New Media Plan requires the following eight activities:

1. Set goals with timelines
2. Develop a measurement plan
3. Create a Content Creation Engine (C.C.E)
4. Align with traditional marketing programs
5. Participate within the community
6. Learn how to help community leaders
7. Build your own online community
8. Analyze and adjust

Set Goals with Timelines

Most marketing plans are built around multiple short-term transient events as opposed to longer-term systematic processes. For example, traditional marketing supports specific events such as product launches, special incentive opportunities, trade shows, and awareness campaigns. Once one of these projects is completed, the marketing staff is reassigned to another event, where they repeat the same series of tasks. New Media Plans are executed differently because their goals are achieved over a longer term. For example, launching a blog is the easy part. It's the constant care and attention it requires that makes it different. New posts must be written, comments must be monitored, and measurements must be made. New Media channels have much longer lifecycles than event-based efforts, and therefore must be measured and managed differently than single-event based activities.

A common mistake is setting traditional transient goals such as, "We'll launch six blogs," or "We'll produce two podcasts," or "We'll add online videos to the Web site." Although each of these goals is measurable, they are merely interim milestones on the way toward a larger, unspecified goal. Why should your company start a blog? Is it to respond to the FUD that a competitor is spreading in the marketplace? Is it to be known as an expert in a particular subject? Is it to help the company's online reputation by increasing search engine rankings? All of these goals require a blog to be in place for success, but the blog isn't the end, it's only the beginning.

Another mistake that companies make is setting goals such as "We are going to create a viral video that gets one million hits."

Again, such a goal is indeed measurable, but even if it were successful and reached a million views, what would it really accomplish for you? Perhaps someone from your company captured video of Paris Hilton accidentally spilling a drink on Oprah Winfrey. If that video were published to your corporate Web site, you might actually get a million views, but so what? Would it help the company gain influence in your respective industry? Would it provide a service to help your customers solve their problems? Could there be any business-related benefit to the project? If the New Media goals that your company sets do not meet requirements such as these, go back to the drawing board and try again.

For instance, let's say that your company wants to increase its visibility as a well-respected expert in your industry. One of your milestones is to move the corporate Web site higher in organic search results. The first step is to take a look at the keywords that you listed during the New Media Audit. Consider writing blogs about those subjects. The more you use those keywords legitimately in your blog content, the more the search engines will associate them with your Web site. Such a goal is measurable, and it has a business purpose.

SEO or SEE?

If Search Engine Optimization is a part of your New Media Plan, always remember that transparency is by far the most important ingredient for success online. Never forget that *Google's mission is to organize the world's information and make it universally accessible and useful.* Oppose that mission with tomfoolery and your company risks Search Engine Excommunication.

There are no shortcuts. Although it's true that the more frequently a keyword is found in your content, the more the search engines notice, abuse of this fact opens unnecessary risks. If the search engines think that you are trying to game the system, your company will be sent straight to the penalty box.

Search Engine optimization of New Media content is very easy to achieve if your company follows one simple rule:

Create the best possible content about your subject and the SEO will take care of itself.

If your company has a blog about *gyroscopes*, where it covers the mechanics of, the electronics within, and the different types of gyroscopes, then using the word in every post is not only appropriate, it is necessary. Search engines love that. If on the other hand gyroscopes are tangential to your business and you try to cheat the system by throwing them randomly into your New Media content, beware the consequences.

New Media measurements are different from traditional measurements that need to hit a home run every time at bat. The longer lifecycles of New Media projects put more emphasis on the *right* audience as opposed to the *largest* one. Don't forget about the power of the small audience. If there are only three companies in the world that use a specific part that your company manufactures and the blog about that part only has three RSS subscribers—the three production managers of those three companies—is the blog successful or not?

New Media Tip: Check your New Media plan

When setting New Media goals, ask the following question: What benefit does the company gain if it succeeds in the goal? If the answer involves something that helps a customer, helps your company's online reputation, or garners more influence, then the goal is appropriate.

Develop a Measurement Plan

Once the goals have been established, measurement must be made to determine the progress toward them. At this point, three decisions must be made:

1. What will your company measure?
2. Will it use paid or free tools to gather the data?
3. Will the company dedicate someone to analyze the data gathered?

There are no shortages of things to measure while executing a New Media Plan. In addition to the items measured in Chapter 10, (unique visitors, RSS subscribers, number of comments, number of blog posts, and age of the blog in weeks) additional measurements help paint a much clearer picture:

- The number of inbound links to your Web site
- The number of memes your company is involved in
- The number of online communities it's mentioned in
- The vibrancy of those communities as measured by active members
- The number of bloggers who cover your company
- The number of company mentions found in services such as Twitter, del.icio.us, and Google Blog Search

- Google Trends or Google Insights to see what people are searching for within your industry[80]

Most of these measurements are open to the world and anyone can see them. Very few companies actually monitor—let alone analyze—the results. The companies that do so will have huge competitive advantages over those who don't. Gather the data. Learn from it. Then use it to your advantage.

Create a Content Creation Engine

Companies are very good at creating one-off content such as datasheets, press releases, or tradeshow signage. However, New Media content requires a commitment to create serial content—smaller pieces that are released on a regular basis. Whether it be from an employee who is monitoring and responding to questions in online communities or one of your corporate bloggers, some level of effort is required. Instead of the traditional roller coaster of effort surrounding marketing and public relations events, New Media activities require a baseline level of effort with occasional activity spikes here and there.

New Media Tip: New Media activities are ongoing
New Media activities are what you do between your silly press releases.

New Media content creation—such as blogging—can be a lonely task for employees. Not only are they required to come up with fresh content periodically, but also those in traditional marketing roles may not understand the value of their efforts and question them. These doubts and a constant need to produce more content can wear on New Media content creators without consistent support. A Content Creation Engine is a tool that management can offer to help New Media content producers.

If your company chooses to become its own publisher, then it has also made the commitment to creating serial content. Blogs need new posts. Podcasts need new programs. Online communities need tending. Instead of isolating these online creators, create a place for them to gather to share their experiences. Such a place will give them the opportunities to learn, to bounce ideas off each other, and to collaborate on new content.

---

[80]   Google insights: http://www.google.com/insights/search/#

For example, let's say that you own a chain of restaurants and one of your bloggers writes about desserts. In addition, your company also has an online video program dedicated to cooking entrées. By offering a place for these two independent content creators to meet, you create the potential for all sorts of content possibilities. The dessert blogger might become a guest on the video show. The blogger might write about the experience, creating a marketing opportunity to tell her audience about the episode. Such cross-promotion could boost the viewership for both shows.

One of the most rewarding activities that I instituted at Synopsys was a monthly conference call set on the third Thursday of every month. The call, intended to be a Content Creation Engine, wasn't mandatory, but existed as a calendar placeholder for bloggers to interact with their fellow bloggers. Along with facilitating a discussion, my role was to provide data and analysis that these content creators could use to increase their audiences, share success stories, or learn from other's mistakes. Many times the most interesting New Media stories came out of these calls. The Godwin "Standing Room Only" story emerged when I asked if anyone on the call had been referred to as a blogger first and an employee second. Without a venue to ask these questions, that valuable story likely never would have been uncovered.

New Media Tip: The answer might be one unasked question away

Questions are the most powerful device that content creators have. What question haven't you asked today?

Another part of the Content Creation Engine requires you to get your content creators out into the community. At Synopsys, we set up a "Meet the Bloggers" Booth at SNUG, the company's user group meeting. Many customers stopped by just to meet with their favorite bloggers, some of whom had achieved rock star-like recognition. Sometimes it's hard to imagine how much of an impact a New Media creator has on an audience while typing on a keyboard, talking into a microphone, or looking into a camera. Meeting these people face-to-face and hearing how your content is impacting their lives is very motivational, adding more fuel to the Content Creation Engine. If you want to experience something special, be standing close when your corporate bloggers are approached by readers for their autographs!

Align with Traditional Marketing Programs

Companies adopting New Media channels typically make two classic mistakes. Both are based on unintended consequences and both are avoidable.

The first scenario occurs when a *Running with Scissors* employee inadvertently creates a New Media program that runs counter to an ongoing traditional marketing effort. For example, let's say that your marketing team has set up a special product demonstration on the tradeshow floor. Simultaneously, your *Running with Scissors* employee decides do organize a "Meet the Bloggers" event for exactly the same time as the demo, yet the venue is located on the other side of the convention center.

The time arrives and attendance at both events suffers unnecessarily. The tragedy of this situation is that not only could it have been avoided, but if they had been coordinated, the two events could have helped one another. Had the marketing team advertised the demo to the online community, perhaps getting a mention in one or two of the corporate blogs, and the *Running with Scissors* employee had scheduled his meeting immediately prior to the demonstration, the entire group could have been led directly through the tradeshow floor to the demonstration, where they surely would have caught the attention of others. The audiences are the same. It's really important for everyone to be on the same page, which leads us to the second version of the problem.

One of the company's *Traditionals* has gotten word that his boss wants to use New Media technologies with their next product announcement. Instead of creating an integrated plan that harnesses the strengths of each medium, he decides to bolt a New Media piece onto the original plan simply to meet his obligation. He decides to use online video as an adjunct to his press release, but instead of using the unique traits of video as an opportunity to add a new dimension to the story, he places a corporate spokesperson reading prepared text in front of a video camera. The new product is announced, the boring video is posted online, and the *Traditional* has met his obligation. In reality, however, he lost an opportunity to put a human face onto the story that your company is trying to tell and may have opened your company up to online mockery as the video garners negative attention.

New Media channels aren't just "add-ons" to traditional marketing efforts. They provide unique opportunities to tell your stories in a different way. If your company wants to release a video simultaneously with a press release, don't put a person in front of a video camera and have her regurgitating the same content. Seek to find new viewpoints for the story. Interview the product's designer. Have a conversation with an early customer. Show video of your product working in the field. Tap into the power of your Content Creation Engine, using your New Media content producers to tell their sides of the story. By doing so, you'll give your online audiences multiple forms of media to choose from.

Participate within the Community

Selected employees must become valuable members of the communities uncovered during the New Media Audit. They must be trained to participate transparently—a subject that can't be stressed enough. The worst thing that a company can do online is to participate under the guise of being someone else. "Astroturfing" is a term used within New Media circles to describe disingenuous posts created by companies who are masking their true identities. The inclination to Astroturf usually occurs when someone trained in the old economics of influence decides to drop advertising copy into an online conversation under an alias.

"Hey, I just read about this great _____ over at _____. Go check it out! —Kathryn.

As an executive, it's your job to mandate that employees use their real names and their real titles when communicating online. Some community members may complain about your corporate presence, but if your company is seeking to be a good citizen and is working to add to the community rather than taking from it, the complaints will eventually subside. It's common for the most vocal of complainers to be turned completely around as they realize that your employee is a valuable resource as opposed to a corporate shill.

Astroturfing is by far the most dangerous activity that your company can participate in. Get caught and your company will suffer an attack on your brand.

New Media Tip: Astroturfing...don't'!

Nobody in your company is smart enough to get away with astroturfing—so don't even try.

Learn How to Help Community Leaders

During the New Media Audit, your company found communities and leaders. Many of these leaders are content creators themselves, who use text, pictures, sounds, and video to connect with their own audiences. These influential individuals take the form of bloggers or podcasters—or have their own online video programs. They use online community platforms such as Twitter or Facebook, and new services that are cropping up daily to share their views. No matter what New Media channels they choose, online leaders are passionate about what they do.

Your company should help these leaders. Offer them "starter content," building blocks that they can add to. Starter content may come in the form of blog posts, logos, high-resolution photos, and videos—anything that they can use to make their points. Starter content may include access to corporate officers for B2B companies, or contests and coupons for those selling Business-to-Consumer (B2C). Companies that become a part of these leaders' Content Creation Engines can benefit greatly from them. Invite leaders to your monthly conference call—either as guest speakers or as people for your team to collaborate with. By offering a resource for community leaders to tap into, your company will benefit as the word spreads virally. It may be a small virus, but a small virus is still a virus.

For the love of all that's holy, keep your *Traditionals* away from these online leaders, who must be allowed to describe *your* product in *their* words. This is not the time to fuss over the carefully worded descriptions your marketing team developed over margaritas at the corporate retreat. If these community leaders want to change the word "happy" to "glad" while describing your product, please don't stand in their way. Be helpful. Be a resource.

Build Your Online Community

There is one community that your company knows more about than any other: its own. It has years of experience communicating with prospects, customers, investors, and employees. Now it needs to contemplate the creation of online properties where these constituents can gather online. Such online properties might include the corporate Web site or third-party-based pages on MySpace, Facebook, or YouTube.

Deciding whether or not to create an online community requires the same thought process as described in the goal-setting section. What is your company trying to accomplish? *Running with Scissors* employees may push to create something cool; yet if it doesn't add anything of value to the constituents or the company, you must kill it.

Sometimes, a community will already exist to serve your constituents. Make an assessment on whether or not it makes sense to organize disparate groups, as in the Merrimack College example, or to take a back seat and participate within an established group rather than starting a new one.

Analyze and Adjust

Online, things move at the speed of light and as such, situations can change suddenly. One moment there may be no online activities surrounding your company, and the next, a meme has catapulted your company into the spotlight—either increasing your influence or adding to your heartburn. Your pilot light might flare into a kitchen fire if no one is there to catch it. The key is to be on the alert. Watch the data. Listen to your online analysts. Look for patterns and make both strategic and tactical adjustments along the way.

Wrapping It Up

By now you should have a good idea for what New Media is all about. You understand:

- How the new economics of influence creates ramifications for corporate communications
- How new online communications channels with no barrier to entry are shifting the publishing industry

- How and why traditional corporate communications content doesn't fit within New Media channels
- How these new channels threaten old assumptions and therefore are likely to instigate a range of reactions—from healthy skepticism to violent resistance
- How to make decisions about whether or not these new channels will work within your company
- Why these new technologies require support from upper level management in order to implement these programs successfully
- How to measure the effectiveness of these New Media efforts

The adoption of New Media channels into your company promises to be a challenging, yet exciting, effort. It will help you connect with customers in ways that were impossible just a few years ago. It will cause upheavals—both inside and outside of the corporate firewall—but when all is said and done, the proper use of New Media channels will bring you closer to your customers.

New Media is not about spending money; it's about how you spend your time. It requires that you reevaluate the efforts of all your employees and determine the best allocation of resources to meet the needs of the new economics of influence. The decisions will be difficult. Those wedded to the old economics of influence won't go down without a fight.

You've got the tools. Use them well.

Chapter Summary:

- The first thing your company should do is a New Media Audit.
- Listening is low risk.
- Measure everything.
- Analyze the data.
- Develop a New Media Plan.
- Create a content creation engine.
- Seek first to help in your online communities.
- Adjust your plan accordingly.

Selected Bibliography

Anderson, Chris. *The Long Tail: Why the Future of Business Is Selling Less of More*. New York: Hyperion, 2006.

Battelle, John. *The Search: How Google and Its Rivals Rewrote The Rules of Business and Transformed Our Culture*. Ottawa: Portfolio Hardcover, 2005.

Brand, Stewart. *The Media Lab: Inventing the Future at M. I. T.* Boston: Penguin (Non-Classics), 1988.

Freberg, Stan. *It Only Hurts When I Laugh*. New York: Crown, 1988.

Fugere, Brian, Chelsea Hardaway, and Jon Warshawsky. *Why Business People Speak Like Idiots: A Bullfighter's Guide*. New York City: Free Press, 2005.

Gillin, Paul. *The New Influencers: A Marketer's Guide to the New Social Media* [New Influencers -Os]. Sanger: Quill Driver Books, 2007.

Godin, Seth. *Meatball Sundae: Is Your Marketing Out of Sync?* Ottawa: Portfolio Hardcover, 2007.

Godin, Seth. *Tribes: We Need You To Lead Us*. Ottawa: Portfolio Hardcover, 2008.

Hewitt, Hugh. *Blog: Understanding The Information Reformation That's Changing Your World*. Waco, Tx: Thomas Nelson, 2006.

Hunt, Tara. *The Whuffie Factor: Using the Power of Social Networks to Build Your Business*. New York, NY: Crown Business, 2009.

Israel, Shel, and Robert Scoble. *Naked Conversations*. Hoboken, New Jersey: John Wiley & Sons Inc, 2006.

Kaushik, Avinash. *Web Analytics: An Hour a Day*. New York: Sybex, 2007.

Levine, Rick, Christopher Locke, Doc Searls, and David Weinberger. *The Cluetrain Manifesto: The End of Business as Usual*. New York: Perseus Books Group, 2001.

Minsky, Marvin. *Society of Mind*. New York: Simon & Schuster, 1988.

Pilzer, Paul Zane. *Unlimited Wealth: The Theory and Practice of Economic Alchemy*. New York: Crown, 1990.

Pirsig, Robert. *Zen and the Art of Motorcycle Maintenance: An Inquiry into Values* (P.S.). New York: Harper Perennial Modern Classics, 2008.

Scott, David Meerman. *The New Rules of Marketing and PR: How to Use News Releases, Blogs, Podcasting, Viral Marketing and Online Media to Reach Buyers Directly*. New York, NY: Wiley, 2008.

Sernovitz, Andy. *Word of Mouth Marketing: How Smart Companies Get People Talking*. New York: Kaplan Business, 2006.

Tapscott, Don, and Anthony D. Williams. *Wikinomics: How Mass Collaboration Changes Everything*. Ottawa: Portfolio Hardcover, 2007.

Walton, Sam. *Sam Walton: Made in America*. United States and Canada: Bantam, 1993.

Weil, Debbie. *The Corporate Blogging Book: Absolutely Everything You Need to Know to Get It Right*. Ottawa: Portfolio Hardcover, 2006.

Index